MAKING EMAG WORK

COLLEGE LIBRARY

Please return this book by the date stamped below - if recalled, the loan is reduced to 10 days

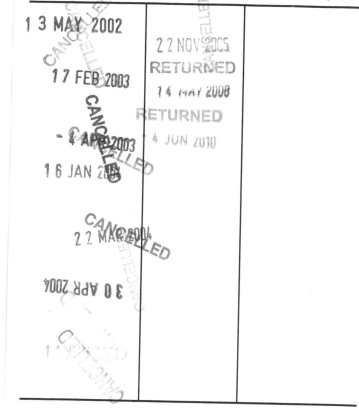

Fines are payable for late return

MAKING EMAG WORK

*Edited by Crispin Jones and
Catherine Wallace*

Trentham Books
Stoke on Trent, UK and Sterling, USA

Trentham Books Limited

Westview House	22883 Quicksilver Drive
734 London Road	Sterling
Oakhill	VA 20166-2012
Stoke on Trent	USA
Staffordshire	
England ST4 5NP	

First published 2001

British Library Cataloguing-in-Publication Data
A catalogue record for this book is available from the British Library

1 85856 230 9

Designed and typeset by Trentham Print Design Ltd., Chester and printed in Great Britain by Biddles Ltd., Surrey.

Contents

Introduction

The introduction of the Ethnic Minority Achievement Grant (EMAG) was a significant step in the current government's attempts to raise levels of achievement for ethnic minorities and this book aims to help make it work effectively. The enlargement of the grant to include Travellers' children (hence EMTAG) created an opportunity to draw in previously neglected groups but also concern that resources would be less clearly targeted. The DfEE has sought to resolve this (Circular on The Standards Fund 2001-2000) by making a seperate grant to Travellers' children; this will be allocated to Local Education Authorities and not, as is EMAG, largely devolved to schools. However, because schools responded to the earlier provision, which included Travellers' children, it is likely that school staff will continue to take account of the wider brief of EMTAG for some time. For this reason this book includes a chapter by Kalwant Bhopal devoted to supporting Gypsy Traveller children in primary and secondary schools.

The EMAG has possibilities for making a real change for the better. However there are also concerns and these are raised by the contributors to this book about a whole range of issues in relation to the groups of pupils they are concerned for. Is the money enough? Clearly not. Are policies to meet targets both clear and practical? A curate's egg is the current answer.

This book indicates how schools can maximise the effectiveness of EMAG but cannot hope to cover all aspects of the grant's intentions. Most of the contributors come from an English as an additional language (EAL) background and the text reflects this. Two areas in particular are only touched on, namely the issue of supporting potentially high-achieving students from ethnic minorities and the wide range of issues relating to African-Caribbean achievement which, we think, merits a book in its own right. But the range of educational backgrounds of the contributors is wide and they have many different concerns. All share a determination to make the grant work – and their contributions indicate to managers and teachers how this might be achieved.

The book is in four related sections. In the first section, Hugh South and Peter Nathan put EMAG in its broader context, South looking at the transition from Section 11 and offering suggestions as to how the effectiveness of the new grant might be enhanced and Nathan looking at the way in which one inner-city LEA has started to use the grant to make a decisive impact upon the achievement levels of ethnic minority children.

The second section relates to a point that South makes: that there are groups of minorities whose specific needs are seldom addressed. This is illustrated in the three chapters on the specific needs of refugee, Gypsy Traveller and Turkish Cypriot children by Jill Rutter, Kalwant Bhopal and Crispin Jones respectively. They show both the common and the unique factors that are currently impeding the educational progress of these three groups of pupils and demonstrate the need for a broader knowledge base about the needs of the many minority groups in UK schools.

The third section concentrates on school and classroom practice from a range of concerns and perspectives. Angela Creese focuses on partnership teaching in the light of her detailed research on this complex practice, Maggie Gravelle considers work relating to the national Literacy Hour with special reference to how this initiative helps bilingual children, while Roger West, taking a critical perspective on EMAG, outlines a range of practice that excludes minority children and contrasts it with practice that is inclusive and effective.

The final section is more forward looking, with Charlotte Franson and Catherine Wallace suggesting ways in which EMAG could fruitfully develop in future years.

This book's genesis was a conference at the Institute of Education organised by the Language Development in Multilingual Schools Initiative, for which the guiding light was Jim Wight. But for illness, Jim would have made an even more significant contribution to the book than he has done. This book is, hopefully, a get well card!

Crispin Jones and Catherine Wallace

Contributors

Kalwant Bhopal is Lecturer in Sociology at Middlesex University

Angela Creese is Lecturer in Linguistics at Leicester University

Charlotte Franson is Lecturer in Education at Birmingham University

Maggie Gravelle is Senior Lecturer in Education at Greenwich University

Crispin Jones is Reader in Education at the Institute of Education, London University

Peter Nathan is Head of Nord-Anglia Hackney Ethnic Minority Achievement Service

Jill Rutter is the National Education Advisor at the Refugee Council

Hugh South is Head of the Ethnic Minority Achievement Centre, Watford, Hertfordshire

Catherine Wallace is Senior Lecturer in Education at the Institute of Education, London University and directs the LDMS at the Institute

Roger West is an EMAG consultant and member of the LDMS, Institute of Education, London University

1

Section 11 to EMAG:
a critical perspective

Hugh South

Introduction

This chapter offers a critical perspective on policy issues resulting from the change from Home Office funding under Section
11 of the Local Government Act 1966 to the DfEE administered Ethnic Minority and Traveller Achievement Grant (EMAG)
and, since autumn of 2000, to EMAG – with a separate grant for
Travellers. It seeks to show that the discourse about policy should
reflect:

- the diversity of needs and provision

- a principled approach to the use of funding

- the involvement of communities and practitioners in policy-
  making

- the role of school action plans as a tool for managing provision

Whatever policies are adopted by future governments, the UK will
continue to be affected by significant changes in world migration
patterns. For the foreseeable future, the education system will need
to be able to respond proactively to pupils entering schools from an
increasingly wide range of backgrounds and at different ages, many
of whom do not speak English as their first language. The United

Nations High Commissioner for Refugees (UNHCR) makes clear that the proportion of displaced persons in the world has increased from approximately 4 million people in the early 1980s to 27 million today (UNHCR, 1997). This huge growth in migration is a continuing trend, and it is not related only to poverty or to displaced persons. Mobility is also a feature of high-status work situations in economically developed countries: the Organisation for Economic Co-operation and Development (OECD, 1998) has calculated that by 2020 some 15 per cent of the population of Frankfurt will be people who do not expect to live there for more than five years (Lo Bianco: 1999). To meet the educational needs of children who enter the system as a result of this accelerating trend in migration, both long-term funding and a substantial training programme are required to ensure that high-quality provision is available. While a primary function of the educational response should be the teaching and learning of English as an additional language (EAL), this needs to be conceived more broadly in terms of home and community language provision, race equality and the role schools can play in altering the relations of power in society.[1]

Contextualising EMAG: the complexity of variables

Discussion of EMAG needs to take into account the national context in which there has been increasing recognition of issues relating to ethnic minority pupil achievement[2] and also the diversity of pupils, posts and school contexts. The number of variables not only makes the whole field complex, but also means that generalisations should be treated with caution. Effective strategies need to be evaluated in the light of particular school circumstances.

Tables 1.1 and 1.2 set out the main areas and types of post funded under EMAG.

It should also be noted that school population profiles are dynamic and each context has particular characteristics, reflecting the number or percentage of ethnic minority pupils, family background and circumstances, and both group and individual learner characteristics.

The number or percentage of ethnic minority pupils is a continuum, with schools which have very small numbers of 'isolated' pupils at

Table 1.1 Specialised interrelated areas supported by EMAG

English as an additional language (EAL)

African-Caribbean pupil achievement

Mentoring

Bilingual support

Home-school liaison and Family Literacy

Outreach

Refugee pupils

Management and administration

Training

(Traveller education – included in the Grant from 1998-2000)

Table 1.2 Types of EMAG post-holder contracts

Posts within team/department (school contract)

Single post – full-time or part-time (school contract)

Buy-back post in single school (LEA contract)

Buy-back post in more than one school (LEA contract)

Peripatetic (LEA contract)

School and LEA contracts combined

Centrally funded posts (LEA)

one extreme, and schools with more than 90 per cent of pupils from ethnic minority backgrounds at the other. Whatever the number of ethnic minority pupils in a school, those with language-learning needs are likely to fall into one of the following broad categories suggested by Leung and Harris:

a) new arrivals: pupils newly migrated to Britain with little or no English language proficiency or familiarity with contemporary British cultural and educational practices

b) pupils born and brought up in Britain but entering early years schooling with overwhelming spoken use of community language but a low level of English language proficiency

c) pupils born and brought up in Britain who are competent and confident users of local British vernacular 'Englishes' and entirely familiar with contemporary British cultural and educational practices, but have difficulties in reproducing accurate and fluent written Standard English in the preferred written genres favoured in specific school disciplines.

d) pupils arriving in Britain for the first time sometime between the ages of 5 and 16, and progressing over a period from a) to c)

e) pupils of Caribbean descent who perhaps constitute a special case of c)

f) pupils who represent an untapped potential for high bi/multilingual competence starting from a substantial family- and community-based confidence and proficiency in speaking a community language (Leung and Harris 1997, p. 10)

Such broad categories relating to learning needs, as well as numbers of ethnic minority pupils, combine with family background and circumstances to contribute to the characteristics of school profiles. For example, they may include:

4

- one, two or three established and predominant ethnic minority communities, such as those seen in Tower Hamlets in London, or in Birmingham,

- wide variations of linguistic, cultural, economic and ethnic backgrounds, as seen in some inner urban and suburban schools

- short-term stay pupils, for example children accompanying international business families

- refugee and asylum seeking pupils

Clearly, the diversity of ethnic minority pupils in the education system is greater than the diversity within the majority group population. Such factors as prior education and literacy experience, age on entry and linguistic, cultural, social and economic backgrounds are important, as is the way these factors impact on learning. A further factor is the influence of individual differences in attitude to learning, learning style, home support and so forth.[3] As a consequence, the combinations of variables which make up the ethnic minority profiles of different schools may call for quite different strategies in response to the particular make-up of the school population.

There has been a tendency to overgeneralise in much of the discourse about ethnic minority pupil achievement and there is a need for evaluative studies which compare schools with similar profiles, and which take account of the complex variables which influence the quality of ethnic minority pupils' educational experience. 'Ethnographic research suggests that Asian pupils' school experiences may vary according to the ethnic composition of their schools' (Gillborn and Gipps, 1996, p. 57).[4] Effective use of EMAG is therefore likely to be context-specific and it may well be that devolution of the grant to schools will assist localised, targeted use of the resource in flexible ways. However, strategic effectiveness depends upon high-quality analysis of information about pupils and rigorous evaluation of work undertaken.

The use of funding: principles and issues

Two of the key guiding concepts in the government's management of social institutions in recent years have been the principles of partnership and devolution. The partnership principle was embedded in the Single Regeneration Budget (SRB), for example. The introduction of Local Management of Schools (LMS) and Fair Funding are both examples of the application of the principle of devolution which brings with it increased institutional responsibility and accountability, together with increased powers. In a delegation to the then Under-Secretary of State for Education, Charles Clarke, in 1998, the National Association for Language Development in the Curriculum (NALDIC) and the Northern Association of Support Services for Equality and Achievement (NASSEA) argued that the concept of partnership should be applied in the particular case of additional funding to support the achievement of ethnic minority pupils in schools. However, it was the principle of devolution which determined the key change from Section 11 to EMAG.

While this book is primarily concerned with the potential of EMAG to raise achievement, provision needs to be seen in the context of the dangers expressed about current policy. These were voiced by community groups and by professional organisations in the period leading to the changes announced in November 1998. NALDIC and NASSEA, for example, set out principles for the use of funding and highlighted some of the dangers. Four of the key principles are discussed below.

1. **Funding should not be devolved to schools**

   This issue was central to the debate. The NALDIC/NASSEA papers referred to the acknowledged concerns about past abuse of Section 11 funding and also to those local authorities which had attempted a form of devolution without success before reverting to a centrally organised strategy.

   Difficulties encountered related to: accurate and equitable assessment of need, staff quality and expertise, appropriate teaching for pupils at all stages of English, effective monitoring and evaluation, flexibility to meet changing needs, and correct use of grant-funded staff time against other competing pressures in school (such as class cover time and SEN support). (NALDIC and NASSEA, 1996, p. 4)

References were also made to the Australian experience where mainstreaming of language funding provided an excuse to abandon all affirmative action and ethnic-specific programmes, including ESL instruction in schools. 'The number of TESOL specialists in schools declined, ESL programmes in a number of states were savagely cut ... mainstreaming began to be seen as a return to assimilation in another guise' (Davison, 1993, p. 17). It is too soon to know if the fears about devolving funding to schools were well founded, but it is one of the reasons why monitoring and evaluation of EMAG is important.

An additional concern about devolution of funding was that it might lead to a loss of the important distinctions between learning English as an additional language (EAL) and literacy development in the context of the National Literacy Strategy, between EAL and SEN, and between teaching and learning EAL and race equality work (NALDIC and NASSEA, 1996). It is not yet clear if the management of EMAG by schools will support the ongoing development of EAL as a specialist area of education, or whether it will lead to a gradual loss of direction and specificity in the use of funding.

2. **There should be long-term stability of funding**
    The DfEE may maintain EMAG as a long-term funding programme but its positioning within the Standards Fund, which has conventionally operated on a 3-year cycle related to current priorities, suggests that the commitment to the long term which practitioners and communities sought has not been secured. Without such commitment, the effects of continuing instability are likely to undermine recruitment and retention of staff and therefore the quality of provision. Loss of expertise has been a major concern in the transition from Section 11 to EMAG. The issue of long-term funding is discussed more fully below.

3. **Funding should be targeted and increased**
    The speed with which the virement to schools has been introduced has not created confidence in the DfEE's intention to maintain EMAG as a specific, targeted grant to further the achievement of ethnic minority pupils. Current plans to rationalise the Standards Fund have led to further uncertainty

about future use of the grant. In 1992/93, government expenditure on Section 11 was £130m. £55m was taken out of Section 11 in the mid 1990s and incorporated in the Single Regeneration Budget (SRB), a fund which reduces over its seven-year duration. DfEE expenditure on EM(T)AG in 2000/01 is £92.25m. Figures on expenditure can be represented in different ways, but it seems clear that there has been a reduction in government expenditure in real terms, while at the same time the uses of the Section 11 and EM(T)AG grants were widened. The withdrawal of Travellers into a separate funding programme somewhat sharpens the focus for 2001.

An additional factor influencing funding stability has been an increase in local government share of expenditure. In 1992 the ratio of central government and local authority funding was 75 per cent: 25 per cent. The ratio now stands at 58 per cent: 42 per cent. Changes in the ratio of funding announced in 1992 used the notion of a 'minimum spend' for local authorities. The amount of grant within a local area became dependent on the local authority's ability to increase its contribution. Ostensibly the increase in local authorities' contributions has risen from £25m in 1988 to £70.25m in 2000/01. The uncertainty about funding at both national and local levels has inevitably influenced the quality of provision.

4. **Monitoring and accountability should build on established Home Office practice**

Concern about misuse of funding stems not only from historic cases of misuse but also from the recognition that whereas Section 11 projects had a single clear responsibility to deliver the service for which they were accountable, schools now have a wide range of demands on their budgets and this creates constant pressures to vire funding (and staff) for various purposes. Monitoring requires clear criteria and an effective mechanism. Given the wider range of purposes for which funding can be used under EMAG, appropriate use is open to interpretation. At the same time, monitoring will be largely retrospective and dependent on school development advisers (in many authorities) and OFSTED inspectors, for both of whom EMAG will be a relatively minor aspect of a much wider brief. The LEA Code of Practice, which promotes intervention in proportion to success and 'light touch' monitoring, restricts the powers of local authorities to influence schools' use of the grant. It is not clear, therefore, how effective monitoring of EMAG will be achieved. In this context, school action plans could make an important contribution. These are further discussed below.

The need for long-term funding

Recognition of the long-term need to relate educational provision to statistics on migration (referred to above) has not been a feature of debate about EMAG. Rather, the focus has been on the achievement of existing ethnic minority pupils in the system triggered by the OFSTED report, *Recent Research on the Achievements of Ethnic Minority Pupils* (Gillborn and Gipps, 1996). Research was reported which showed both high and low achievement within ethnic minority groups. The below-average levels of attainment of Bangladeshi, Pakistani and African-Caribbean groups revealed in research studies have been a matter for particular concern. The thrust of the government drive which followed publication of the Gillborn and Gipps report[5] was primarily concerned, therefore, with the achievement of three long-established communities making up a very high percentage of the ethnic minority pupil population. However, some schools are equally concerned about other smaller groups such as pupils of Turkish and Somali origin (OFSTED, 1999, para. 28) and those who are refugees and asylum-seekers from a variety of backgrounds.[6] There is still a relative lack of research data which show the patterns of achievement of these and other ethnic minority groups in schools. The lesson to be learned from this situation is not only that EMAG needs to work in concert with the whole education system to set accelerated targets to raise the attainments of these groups, but that long-term funding should be seen as integral to policies which attempt to address the long-established below-average educational achievement of these and other groups.

Despite the years of funding instability and uncertainty in Section 11 provision, service delivery through the concept of 'projects' brought relative cohesion. 'Projects' offered the potential for developing professional identity and a common understanding of effective practice. This is not to suggest that all projects were as effective as schools would have wished, although the evidence from a substantial body of OFSTED reports[7] shows that much of the work undertaken by staff funded by Section 11 was of a high quality. The point at issue is that if the relative cohesion of the 'project' structure is acknowledged, EMAG can be seen as exploding the Section 11 mould, bringing the potential for increased diversification in the use of the funding. It was clear that the DfEE was uncomfortable with a source of funding that incorporated its own agenda and was not solely and explicitly driven by the government's agenda for raising standards and more importantly by the belief that schools should have maximum determination in the use of their funds. The DfEE's intention was primarily to ensure that schools took responsibility for raising the achievement of their ethnic minority pupils by harnessing the funding to their own planning and target setting in line with the national agenda for driving up standards.[8] The effect of devolving funds to schools, together with their responsibility for determining the use of their EMAG budget within the broad constraints set by the DfEE, has given the opportunity for provision to be brought fully within schools' agendas: the question is whether this will lead to improved quality of provision for ethnic minority pupils. This question cannot be taken for granted and there is a need for studies which offer objective evidence of the impact of the funding changes on provision. Two exercises have been planned, one by HMI and one commissioned by the DfEE. The findings from these studies will be significant since they are likely to be the only means of evaluating the transition.

Communities, practitioners and policy makers

One of the changes introduced in the 1986 circular on Section 11 was that 'there must be consultation with representatives of the intended beneficiaries of the special provision' (Home Office, 1989, p. 34). Together with the requirements that post-holders should be identifiable, have a job description and that there must be clear arrangements for monitoring performance, this was a response to widespread concerns expressed by communities and within the education system about abuse of funding.[9] The requirement to consult with communities was maintained when further changes were introduced in 1992. Many Section 11 projects took this responsibility very seriously and saw themselves as directly accountable to local communities. The closer links established with local communities led to strong community support for maintaining Section 11 projects when funding reductions were threatened by government and local authorities during the 1990s.

There is a significant change of emphasis in relation to consultation with communities under the EMAG arrangements determined by the DfEE. Section B17.11 of the Standards Fund 2000-2001 document requires local authorities to consult with communities if they are 'drawing up or updating their action plan' or making 'an alteration'. There is no ongoing requirement to consult with communities if these conditions do not apply, nor is there any requirement for schools, as the recipients of the devolved grant, to consult with relevant communities or ethnic minority parents on their use of the additional funding. This contrasts with the requirements for the submission of projects for Section 11 funding, which required detailed information about community organisations, the process of consultation and the response of communities. 'Client groups and other relevant organisations should be consulted as part of the objective and target setting process and monitoring the effectiveness of an ongoing project' (Home Office, 1990a, para. 4.6).

Consultation with communities has therefore been weakened. Since there has been no official explanation or acknowledgement of a constructive role for communities, it is only possible to offer a tentative interpretation. A generous construction would be not that the DfEE wishes to overlook the role of communities but rather that ethnic minority pupils are finally being seen as integral to the school population: the old association of Section 11 with 'immigrants' – outdated and unacceptable for the past 25 years – has been swept aside. This interpretation would suggest that the needs of ethnic minority pupils are part of, rather than distinct from, the drive to raise standards in schools. In many ways the shift that such a construction implies is long overdue: the success of some children from ethnic minority communities should be taken on board by the whole education system, of which EMAG is a part, and the need to build in a level of accountability to such communities as a special case might be thought to be no longer appropriate. However, the position of the communities and of ethnic minority pupils is not a peripheral matter and EMAG should not be seen as in any way implying that it is; it remains specific, targeted funding, and communities have a right to know and should be able to influence how it is being used. The history of Section 11 bears out this position: 'Communities argued that while large sums of money were being given to local authorities the communities felt no benefit' (Home Office, 1989, p. 10). Although consultation with communities is not seen as having a significant influence on policy, schools, local authorities and the DfEE would be wise to take account of the past concerns:

> It is vitally important that there is accountability to minority communities built into the arrangements for funding – this is specific in the Home Office brief which is not the case with other government departments or agencies. (NALDIC and NASSEA, 1998, p. 6)

There is, of course, no reason why schools with devolved budgets, as well as LEAs, should not develop arrangements for involving local communities. However, there is little evidence that schools have responded to having control of the budget by taking it as a matter of principle that they should consult with their ethnic minority parents about how they plan to use the funding. Since guidance from the DfEE does not require this and since the perspectives of communities are not necessarily consistent with those of schools, it seems likely that the voice of communities will diminish and with it any influence they may have had over the use of the funding.

Community involvement is not only a policy-making issue. It is also essential to make inclusive education a reality. For example, a fundamental belief in early years education is to build on children's experience, as the QCA has confirmed (QCA, 1999). This principle, of course, extends beyond the early years and it is one which teachers of EAL explicitly acknowledge (NALDIC, 1999). The application of this principle through planning classroom teaching is a vital component of effective practice to ensure ethnic minority pupils' achievement. However, when teachers do not share the cultural and linguistic experience of children's home experience, strategies to bridge the gap between home, community and school, and to extend understanding, need to be developed. The experiences and perspectives of ethnic minority parents and communities therefore need to be better understood and utilised by schools and policy-makers alike.

Practitioners and the process of policy-making

Just as there is a need for structured ways in which communities should be able to influence the use of funding at school, local authority and national levels, so also the voice of practitioners needs to influence policy making. The history of failure to give national recognition to EAL, bilingualism and race equality in education has led practitioners to feel disempowered, particularly in recent years during the transition to EMAG. For example, their participation in the consultation exercise carried out jointly by the Home Office and the DfEE in January 1988 did not appear to influence decision-making, which was not made transparent through publication of the results of the exercise. This contrasts with the review of Section 11 in 1998 which resulted in a report setting out the arguments presented in the consultations and explaining the policy decisions taken (Home Office, 1989). Equally, at the local authority level, reorganisation to comply with EMAG within a very short time generally involved decision making at Director or Assistant Director level. Rightly or wrongly, those who understood the field at first hand had little say in the decision-making process.

> There is a very problematical idea of democracy that the kind of knowledge that petitioners in any field – health or education – have needs to be *overwritten* by a class of professional policy advisers who convert teachers' knowledge about teaching, or health practitioners' knowledge about health practice, into a science of policy making for ministers. In other words teachers often feel that policy texts disempower them, remove their experience, their knowledge and their wisdom, partly because of this process of overwriting, and partly also because there is a notion that the lived experience of practice is an inappropriate description of reality for the making of decisions. So if we understand the belief in governments that there is a need for a professional class of advisers who actually produce 'objective, tech-

nical, scientific' knowledge, you see what that does about our field. It says that we cannot be 'objective', that we are 'subjective' – in other words that our kinds of claims are motivated or interested by some self-serving purpose whereas theirs, whoever 'they' are, are not. They are motivated by technical, objective or non-ideological ways of being. (Lo Bianco, 1999)

While practitioners understand the reality of the political contexts in which they work, Lo Bianco's words will resonate with the recent experience of many of them. However, it is important to recognise that policy derives from discourse. Practitioners and communities need to take steps to ensure that they engage in this process, and policy makers need to consider whether they have created the necessary structures to enable practitioners and communities to be genuine participants in the discourse.

School action plans: a tool for change

Within the areas of education funded through EMAG there are specific specialisms: African-Caribbean pupil achievement, teaching and learning English as an additional language, bilingual teaching in classrooms, support for refugees and asylum-seekers, home-school liaison, family literacy and outreach work and, until autumn 2000, Traveller education. More work needs to be done on making explicit the commonalities of these special areas and the relationship between them, as well as what is distinctive about each one. However, in the strategic management of EMAG, the school action plan is a key tool.

The funding that has been devolved to schools is specific targeted funding. Local authorities have a responsibility for ensuring that the funding is used appropriately and that this is monitored. LEAs are therefore entitled to ask schools to provide data about pupil needs and achievements and to say how they intend using the funding. The school action plan is therefore an important mechanism for LEAs to gather the data they need for their own action plan, which is required by the DfEE, and to carry out their responsibilities for monitoring the use of funding. But just as importantly, the action plan is an essential tool for school planning purposes. The elements that might be required in an action plan include:

- data collection and analysis to

    provide an assessment of needs

    discriminate between groups

    provide an overview

    feed into evaluation and year-on-year progress

- objectives for different groups and target setting
- identification of strategies including

    a rationale

    a timescale

    planning and review

    school and classroom levels

    evaluation and dissemination

    professional development

- utilisation of posts
- consultation with parents/community
- related activities through other funding (e.g. SRB)

In addition action plans should:

- involve EMAG staff and senior management working to-gether
- be linked to the School Development Plan
- lead to an annual review by EMAG staff
- be a tool for evaluation by the school and monitoring by the LEA
- involve an external evaluator where new strategies are being trialled

Although the DfEE has not demanded that schools complete action plans,[10] they should be required by local authorities as the best mechanism to encourage effective use of the budget which is devolved to schools and to provide a handle for monitoring purposes. Schools may not welcome additional bureaucracy, but if the EMAG action plan is linked to the School Development Plan, it can be seen as an integral part of school planning, and can provide schools with a means of discussing their strategy for using their earmarked funding with parents, communities and governors, all of whom have a right to enquire and participate.

Recommendations

It has already been emphasised that the areas of education funded through EMAG are complex, and since they have been given little official recognition until recently, there is a need to increase understanding. One way this can be achieved is through documented evaluations of EMAG practice from within schools, through the monitoring functions of LEAs and OFSTED inspection teams, and through independent studies commissioned by the DfEE. Both quantitative and qualitative studies will be needed. A second equally important way is through an extensive programme of training, for both mainstream and specialist teachers. Substantial additional funding would be required to support such a programme, which is beyond the scope of EMAG itself.

In addition to the policy issues raised in this chapter, each area funded through EMAG has specific developments that need to be considered. A mechanism is needed to draw these together. While it would be impossible to list them here, some general recommendations arise from the considerations addressed in this chapter:

- Mechanisms are needed for involving communities and practitioners in policy-making processes; both of these groups need to ensure that they engage in the discourse.

- Further consideration needs to be given to how EMAG will be monitored.

- Virement of EMAG funding should be withdrawn.

- A date for a policy review should be set. The process should be transparent and it should take account of projections for future migration patterns, long-term funding needs, and the evidence of the effectiveness of the current policy for funding ethnic minority pupil achievement.

- Further work is needed to clarify what is distinctive about the different specialist areas funded through EMAG and what they have in common, in order to produce a conceptual framework to support understanding, planning and evaluation.

- A strategy is required for evaluating and disseminating practice – this should take account of the different specialist areas funded through EMAG, and should include management.

- School EMAG action plans should be required, to enhance planning, evaluation and monitoring.

- Studies are needed which explore effective strategies in schools with similar ethnic minority pupil profiles.

- A major training programme is required to give all headteachers and teachers a basic understanding of areas relating to ethnic minority pupil achievement, including EAL, bilingualism and race equality, and to make possible the accreditation of specialist qualifications. This requires a substantial separate funding initiative.

- A code of practice should be established relating to additional support for ethnic minority pupils.

It is to be hoped that these recommendations will be followed so that the new grant can achieve its aim, and that the educational achievements and inclusion of all children can be enhanced in our schools.

2

Carpe diem: responding to the Ethnic Minority Achievement Grant – a perspective from an inner London borough

Peter Nathan

This chapter outlines how the London Borough of Hackney has reacted to the challenge of the introduction of the much awaited EMAG. It is my view that it is important that Ethnic Minority Achievement (EMA) teams 'seize the day', taking hold of the opportunities presented to them, particularly in the new monitoring and evaluation role identified in the government EMAG circular, which will inevitably be combined with support, advice and training. Otherwise LEA services will be failing and could allow the worst excesses of Section 11 to come back and haunt us like Marley's ghost, with teachers being used for cover, poor staff pushed into the support role and much other malpractice.

Section 11 – a potted history

I think, though, that it is important to reflect on that past history of Section 11 to understand why this change was necessary. Section 11 funding began as a response to the growing racial tensions of the 1950s and 1960s with a number of high-profile and well-remembered riots such as the one at Notting Hill in 1958, and also the infamous Smethwick by-election in 1964, when the Conservative slogan 'If you want a nigger for a neighbour, vote Labour' was used.

Perhaps most significant of all was Enoch Powell's infamous 'rivers of blood' speech. Section 11 of the 1966 Local Government Act was quickly rushed through Parliament as a result of this heightening of the political temperature and provided local authorities with the opportunity to apply for grants if they had a 'presence within their areas of substantial numbers of immigrants ...from the Commonwealth' (NUT, 1978, p. 5). A speech in the House of Commons by Roy Hattersley MP reflects the view of the time in it he states:

> I hope that when the money under Section 11 is distributed, the Secretary of State will bear in mind that as well as providing smaller English classes in which English can be adequately taught, as well as providing extra visitors to parents to remind them of their obligations in Britain, it is essential to teach these children basic British customs, basic British habits and, if one likes, basic British prejudices (quoted in Dorn and Hibbert, 1987, p. 61).

The view was that these foreigners or immigrants had to become stereotypically British or English, although there was no attempt to define this as Prime Minister John Major attempted to do in the 1990s, identifying concepts such as warm beer and cricket on the village green.

The fact that funding came from the Home Office meant that there was no real understanding of the educational issues involved. There was no direct policy lead or guidance from the Home Office at that time and therefore local responses varied considerably. Funding was based on a bidding process and not on a needs analysis. Furthermore, there was no proper monitoring system of how allocated funding was used or indeed any understanding of how it might best be used to meet the needs of ethnic minority communities. This led to much funding abuse – abuse in the sense that the funds provided were not spent on the needs of the target group but instead were used as part of the pool of the education spend, for example, or to reduce class sizes.

In the 1980s and 1990s, the Home Office did tighten up its monitoring of grant use, and guidance was provided to ensure that monies were better targeted. But there were still considerable problems at a local level. A key issue was that 'Section 11' teams in some LEAs

were used as dumping grounds for staff who could not
elsewhere. These would include teachers who perhaps
ceived as being unable to teach a whole class but able to w
small groups of children! This flew against the EAL-teaching ideology of the time, which focused on partnership or joint whole-class
teaching, a view also reflected in the Swann report which recom-
mended such an advisory role for EAL teachers (DES, 1985).
Section 11 teams in some LEAs were a convenient way to place un-
placeable teachers – this represented a very clear example of institutional racism.[12]

EMAG – a new opportunity?

The Ethnic Minority Achievement Grant for the first time gives a
direct lead from the government department responsible for education on how erstwhile Section 11 monies should be spent. Circular
13/98 states that the funding is for supporting pupils for whom
English is an additional language and for raising the achievement of
all ethnic minority pupils who are at risk of underachieving. The
grant, renamed EMAG as from April 2000, also included meeting
the needs of refugee and Traveller pupils. This is the first time a clear
and unambiguous statement has been made about the use of these
monies. The circular also identifies specific responsibilities for
schools and LEAs, including a target-setting agenda for specific
ethnic groups. It indicates a desire to move towards a needs-based
formula at a national level for funding distribution. These changes
do appear to present quite an opportunity to move forward in terms
of meeting the needs of ethnic minority children in schools, particularly as the circular also requires schools to have their own EMAG
action plans and to ensure that training is available for all staff.

Yet although there is much good in the new plans, there are a number
of areas of real concern. A key requirement of the grant is the
devolving of funding to schools, thus potentially weakening the
control of LEAs on how the funds are used. It is well known that
some special-needs funding already delegated to school budgets is
not always used for its intended purpose and the fear is that the same
will happen to EMAG funds. Furthermore, because school EMAG
budgets may fluctuate from year to year based on need defined by a

local formula, which is a further grant requisite, there may be considerable job insecurity and the use of temporary contracts. This may lead to the de-professionalisation of the field of EAL and to this area of work being seen as having low status and being without a proper career structure. If the emphasis is on devolving more and more funds to schools, then a question has to be asked concerning the future of central LEA services and the expertise that can be offered to schools. One of the essential ways, I believe, to ensure that these central teams do survive is through the monitoring and evaluating role provided for LEAs in the grant criteria. I will explore this in the next section, while also looking at the local context of Hackney.

The local context

The London Borough of Hackney is one of the poorest parts of the United Kingdom, having very high levels of economic deprivation. It also has a long and proud history of being home to large numbers of refugees from all over the world. Indeed, my father's parents came to Hackney at the turn of the century from Lublin in southern Poland (then Russia), escaping from the pogroms, an earlier form of ethnic cleansing. Today, some 50 per cent of Hackney pupils are bilingual, with over 80 languages spoken in its 74 schools. The main minority languages are Turkish, Yoruba and Bengali, although many other languages are spoken by sizeable minorities. A further 20 per cent of the school population are of Caribbean heritage and 10 per cent of pupils are classified as 'other'. The level of achievement of Hackney pupils compared to national averages is not high and there are particular problems about the achievement at secondary school of Turkish-speaking pupils and Caribbean boys.

Hackney has also been beset with political problems affecting the management of the LEA. This in part led to a damning OFSTED report on the LEA in 1997; the report identified the Section-11-funded Language and Learning Service as extremely poor. The service suffered from a legacy of staffing problems, confused management systems, lack of proper data collection procedures, little community involvement and unworkable disciplinary and capability procedures.

An opportunity to change the agenda at a local level

In contrast to a number of other local authorities, Hackney strongly welcomed the introduction of EMAG because in many ways it presented the opportunity for a new or 'fresh' start in meeting ethnic minority pupils' needs. The nine key changes that were implemented are identified below:

1. The change in grant remit allowed the central LEA Language and Learning Service to be restructured with a virtually complete personnel change in the management team.

2. A new clear formula was developed for allocating EMAG funds to schools.

3. A proper statistical data-collection system was introduced for EAL fluency levels, language and ethnicity. A moderation system was used to ensure that the EAL fluency levels assigned by schools were accurate.

4. A headteachers' and governors' working party was set up to oversee the changes.

5. The new, renamed Ethnic Minority Achievement Service (EMAS) set up a high-quality training programme including joint working with the literacy and numeracy teams.

6. The EMAS team required all schools to have EMAG action plans in place by the end of July 2000.

7. Funding was completely devolved to schools, with a pool created for staff not required by schools.

8. Clear targets were set for ethnic minority achievement within the LEA EMAG action plan, the education development plan and in the most recent post-OFSTED action plan.

9. The head of EMAS was placed on the Education Department senior management team (SMT).

These changes have allowed the new EMAS to have a high profile in the LEA and have put EMA issues firmly on the local educational agenda.

The EMAG action plan

A key document outlining the way forward has been the EMAG action plan. This has meant that at both LEA and individual school levels, targets have to be set for the achievement of specific ethnic minority groups. The action plan also identifies six key areas for action until 2002, the period for which the grant is initially funded. These include looking at:

- induction and admission arrangements for new-arrival bi-lingual children and refugees

- appointing EMA governors and defining their role

- reducing exclusions of ethnic minority pupils

- training for staff on EAL and achievement issues

- clarifying the needs of pupils with EAL and SEN

- building strong links with parents and community organisations

The EMAG monitoring and evaluation visit or audit

A critical role for LEA EMA services is to monitor the effectiveness of grant use through a monitoring and evaluating audit of schools. In Hackney, a procedure is being developed to support schools with self-evaluation, to identify what they are doing effectively and what the next steps should be in addressing achievement issues. A two-page list of questions or *aide-mémoire* (see Appendix to this chapter) has been devised after consultation with schools, governors and elected members. It is split into five sections covering areas critical for achievement, such as ethnic monitoring, quality assurance, how the grant is targeted, financial monitoring, training and any other areas that are relevant to the school. (It is interesting to look at this *aide-mémoire* alongside that of Jim Wight in the Appendix to Chapter 4 below.)

The audit visit consists of a scrutiny of record-keeping, planning and other relevant documentation, an interview with the headteacher and/or EMA co-ordinator and lesson observations of EMAG-funded staff. A summary report with agreed recommendations is provided for the headteacher. Many schools have welcomed this approach. Schools will be visited every two to three years, although more frequent follow-up visits may be needed in some cases. It is hoped that this approach, along with the other previously mentioned changes, will empower headteachers and EMAG-funded staff to succeed in raising ethnic minority achievement.

Will it be successful?

I believe that EMAG will only be successful if there is a strong, central LEA service to monitor grant use and provide support and advice to schools. Already, schools are experimenting with the flexibility of the grant-funding regime, using the funds for resources, training and classroom assistants, and they are also experimenting with differing practice. Much of this is to be welcomed, but as was noted at the start of the chapter, funding abuse can always happen and has been alleged at some London schools fairly recently. This is why it is vitally important for LEA EMAS teams to seize the day, to set up secure systems to ensure that the grant works in its purpose of effectively meeting the needs of ethnic minority pupils in our schools.

APPENDIX
London Borough of Hackney: EMAG monitoring and evaluation visit

An EMAG monitoring visit will require a report to be written covering areas identified below as appropriate. Key areas the monitoring visit will cover:

1. Ethnic monitoring

a) Are ethnic groups monitored in terms of attainment?

b) Are there any significant differences between ethnic groups in terms of attainment or rate of progress through EAL stages, and is gender an additional factor?

c) Are EAL pupils language levels recorded and is progression between language levels monitored and updated on a regular basis? What evidence is used to validate language levels? Are they measured against SATs and GCSE results?

d) Are exclusions monitored by ethnicity?

e) Is unauthorised absence monitored by ethnicity?

f) Is the number of ethnic minority pupils on the SEN register monitored by ethnicity and language stage level?

g) Is attendance at parents' afternoons/evenings monitored by ethnicity?

h) Does the school monitor any other areas?

i) Has the school set targets and outcome measures for the achievement of ethnic minority groups in the school? Have these been agreed with the LEA and are they consistent with LEA-wide targets?

2. Targeting of EMAG funds the school receives

a) What is the financial breakdown of the school's allocation?

b) What staffing does the school fund using the grant and how are they timetabled?

26

c) Does most teaching take place within the mainstream classroom, in withdrawal groups or in a mixture of the two?

d) Are the staff used for cover or for general teaching duties?

e) Does the school run induction classes for new arrivals and/or literacy groups?

f) When do EMAG-funded staff meet to plan with class or subject teachers?

g) Do the EMAG-funded staff have resources to enable them to work effectively?

h) Does the targeting of resources reflect the school's EMAG action plan and School Development Plan?

3. Training

a) What training have EMAG-funded staff had in the last year?

b) What training have mainstream staff had on issues concerning raising the achievement of ethnic minority pupils in the past two years?

c) Have EMAG-funded staff had training in the literacy and numeracy strategies?

4. Quality Assurance

a) Are the staff employed through the grant appropriately qualified according to the guidance in the Standards Fund rules?

b) What is the school's expectation in terms of planning and record keeping of EMAG funded staff?

c) How does the school monitor the quality and effectiveness of EMAG funded staff's classroom practice?

d) Does the school have an effective system for admitting and inducting new-arrival ethnic minority children?

e) Does the school have effective support mechanisms in place to support refugee children?

f) What systems does the school have in place to ensure that support to EAL and ethnic minority pupils is effective when EMAG-funded staff are not in the classroom?

The monitoring visit will include classroom observation of EMAG-funded staff and scrutiny of planning and record keeping documentation.

5. Other areas

a) Is the school developing new and innovative projects to meet the needs of ethnic minority pupils?

b) are there other issues that need to be raised or added to the report?

c) Is a follow-up visit required?

3

EMAG and refugee children: perpetuating discrimination?

Jill Rutter

Introduction[13]

There are nearly 19 million asylum-seekers and refugees in the world today, more than at any other time in history: indeed, the number of refugees has doubled in a decade. Their migration is a growing challenge to governments, non-governmental organisations and international agencies. In relation to education alone, there are now approximately 69,000 asylum-seeking and refugee children in UK schools. Their reception is presently a matter of educational debate. In England, the failure of the Ethnic Minority Achievement Grant (EMAG) to deliver support to refugee children, particularly those outside London, is a key component of this debate.

The word refugee is now part of everyday vocabulary. But it does have a precise legal meaning. A person with refugee status is defined as someone who has fled from his or her home country, or is unable to return to it, according to the UN definition, 'owing to a well-founded fear of being persecuted for reasons of race, religion, nationality, membership of a particular social group or political opinion'. An asylum-seeker is a person who has crossed an international border in search of safety (and refugee status) in another country. In the UK, asylum-seekers are people who are awaiting a Home Office decision as to whether they can remain.

The legal definition of a refugee is derived from the 1951 UN Convention and the 1967 UN Protocol Relating to the Status of Refugees. These two legal instruments enshrine the rights of asylum-seekers and refugees in international law, preventing them from being returned to countries where they fear persecution.

In order to understand the educational issues that face refugee and asylum-seeking children currently in the UK, it is important to understand the context within which many such pupils live. As a consequence, much of the first half of this chapter explored these vital contextual issues.

Refugees in the UK

Some 71,160 asylum applications were lodged with the Home Office in 1999. The Refugee Council estimate that 14,000 school-aged asylum-seeking children arrived in the UK in 1999. Once an individual or family has arrived in Britain, the immediate concern is to begin the process of applying for political asylum. An asylum application may be lodged at the port of entry, or at the Immigration and Nationality Department of the Home Office, after entry to Britain. On the basis of documentation given to the Immigration and Nationality Department, a decision is made. This can be one of three different outcomes:

- full refugees status (42 per cent of decisions in 1999)

- Exceptional Leave to Remain (ELR) (12 per cent of decisions in 1999)

- a refusal of an asylum application (46 per cent of decision in 1999)

The high proportion of those refused (compared with 16 per cent in early 1993) is a major cause for concern to human rights and refugee organisations. It is part of wide-ranging legislative and policy changes affecting the immigration and social rights of asylum-seekers in the UK. For example, asylum-seekers have experienced major restrictions in their rights to housing and social support. These are described below and, in the opinion of the Refugee Council, will have a major impact on the ability of asylum-seeking children to settle and study in a new school. The new asylum-support arrangements also pose challenges to EMAG-funded EAL services outside London.

New support arrangements for asylum-seekers

As mentioned already, asylum-seekers' rights to public housing have been limited by recent legislation. The Asylum and Immigration (Appeals) Act 1993, the Housing Act 1996 and the Asylum and Immigration Act 1996 restricted asylum-seekers' access to social housing. From 1993, asylum-seekers accepted as homeless by a local authority could only be housed in temporary accommodation and from 1996 were barred from a housing waiting list. These measures have made asylum-seekers a very mobile population. Research conducted by the author in one central London school in 1998 indicated that asylum-seeking children moved home between four and six times during their first two years in the UK. The educational implications of high pupil mobility are significant (Dobson, 1999; Lodge, 1998; Power, et al. 1998). As well as disrupting the already interrupted education of a refugee child, such high pupil mobility has a negative effect on school budgets and the EMAG budget cycle. Teachers spend time settling in asylum-seeking children and then find that they move on in a few weeks. A coherent curriculum is difficult to deliver to a class with a highly mobile pupil population and this affects the stable pupil population too.

Mobility is increasingly being coupled with poverty. In 1987 income support regulations were changed so that asylum-seekers could only claim 90 per cent of the personal allowances of income support. Further changes were implemented in 1996, when the Asylum and Immigration Act 1996 prevented some groups of asylum-seekers from accessing income support.

In 1996 only those asylum-seekers who applied at the port of entry were allowed to claim income support. All 'in-country' applicants and those asylum-seekers appealing against a negative decision lost access to benefits. Instead, they became the responsibility of local authority social services departments. Families with children were supported under the provisions of the Children Act 1989 and given a cash allowance and some form of temporary accommodation. Those asylum-seekers without children were supported under the provisions of the National Assistance Act 1948 (in Scotland, the Children Act (Scotland) and the Social Work (Scotland) Act 1968). This required social services departments to provide sustenance, warmth and shelter – in practice, food vouchers redeemable in a single designated supermarket and temporary accommodation. In England and Wales, case law deemed that giving asylum-seekers a cash allowance was illegal.

What has resulted from all of this is a chaotic system detrimental both to asylum-seekers and to local government. Adult asylum-seekers were left cashless and unable to purchase items such as bus fares, books, clothing and shoes, second-hand goods and even the cheapest forms of entertainment such as a cup of coffee. Local authorities were not fully compensated by central government for the services they provided for destitute asylum-seekers and some local authority officers and councillors began to resent them. Some of the less scrupulous councils briefed the press. Headlines such as 'Influx of refugees costing thousands' (*Kettering Evening Telegraph*, 7 August 1998) or 'Old Folk's Home to be hostel for refugees' (*Harrow Leader*, 16 July 1998) became commonplace. Perhaps most invidious of all, the term 'bogus asylum-seeker' entered the public discourse. The involvement of the local press, as well as most of the national tabloids, undoubtedly created greater public hostility to refugees, which ultimately led to racial violence.

By 1997, there was a shortage of hostel-type accommodation in Greater London for families without access to benefits. London local authorities began to move asylum-seekers out of the capital, often to seaside towns. Cashless, unsupported and with nothing to do, these asylum-seekers were a visible group who attracted more adverse media coverage.

It was in the wake of growing public hostility and concerted lobbying from local authorities that the government was forced to take back responsibility for asylum-seekers. The Immigration and Asylum Act was passed in 1999, amid a further round of negative media coverage. Rather than restore benefits, the Immigration and Asylum Act has introduced a new support system for asylum-seekers, which most refugee agencies believe to be beset with problems and that will condemn asylum-seekers to high levels of stress and isolation.

By July 2000 all new applicants (and refusals in Scotland) will go into the new Home Office support system administered by the National Asylum Support Service (NASS), part of the Immigration and Nationality Directorate of the Home Office. They will receive vouchers and a cash allowance of £10 per person per week. The vouchers, printed by a company called Sodexho, will be posted to an asylum-seeker's home address. The vouchers can be redeemed at named retail outlets but asylum-seekers will not be allowed to receive any change for their purchases. A cash chitty, exchangeable at a post office, will also be posted. The level of support now amounts to less than 70 per cent of an income support level for an adult.

Asylum-seekers without anywhere to stay will also be dispersed out of London and the South East, to the new regional cluster areas. These are:

- South Central
- the South West
- Eastern
- the East Midlands
- the West Midlands
- the North West
- the North East
- Yorkshire and Humberside
- Scotland
- Wales

Most local authorities, although not all, have joined Regional Cluster Areas. There are other local authorities which have stated that they do not wish to host any more asylum-seekers and have thus declined to join Regional Cluster Areas. All Regional Cluster Areas have a lead local authority. The role of the Regional Cluster Areas is to work with NASS to identify accommodation for asylum-seekers.

About 40 per cent of the accommodation will be provided by local authorities and 60 per cent by private landlords. The location of the accommodation will be determined by the availability of housing and of an existing multi-ethnic population and the potential for developing support services.

Any asylum-seeker refusing dispersal will lose all access to support and housing. Moreover, unaccompanied asylum-seeking children will not be supported by the NASS scheme but will remain the responsibility of local authority social services departments under the provisions of the Children Act 1989.

If an asylum-seeker receives a positive decision on his or her application, that asylum-seeker becomes eligible for benefits and is free to move anywhere in the UK. Provided the asylum-seeker has not lived in a particular local authority for more than six months (and thus has a local connection under homelessness legislation), that person is also free to apply for social housing anywhere in the UK.

The effects on children of the NASS scheme

Child care and refugee agencies have highlighted the following concerns about the NASS support scheme:

Stigmatisation

Many asylum-seekers report hostility when they exchange their vouchers at shops; and children who have no toys, television or smart clothes will feel stigmatised at a time in their life when they are most sensitive to peer pressure.

Poverty

The NASS scheme is meant to provide essential living needs only, at a level of 70 per cent of income support for adults and 100 per cent for children. But in reality, this level of support will be lower, as asylum-seekers will not receive change for any purchases they make. Asylum-seekers who live in a virtually cashless support system will be excluded from many things that everyone else regards as essential. These include bus fares, haircuts, second-hand goods and anything not provided by retail outlets that accept vouchers. Worse, vouchers have to be spent within one month of issue. Given this requirement, it is impossible for asylum-seekers to save for clothes and new shoes. A parent who needs to travel by bus to accompany a young child to school is unlikely to have access to cash to pay for the journey.

Isolation

Many asylum-seekers are being sent to areas that have no existing refugee communities and report loneliness and isolation as a consequence, factors that make them much more psychologically vulnerable. Except for the big metropolitan areas such as Birmingham and Manchester, there are unlikely to be refugee community organisations in the new Regional Cluster Areas.

Vulnerability to racial attack

Despite the Home Office guidance on the choice of accommodation, many asylum-seekers will end up being housed in areas where there are few other people from visible ethnic minorities. Some of these inevitably will be places of existing tension and high unemployment. Given the hostile attitudes of much local and national print media towards asylum-seekers, the Refugee Council believes that some groups will be very vulnerable to racial abuse and attack. At the time of writing, five weeks after the NASS system was introduced, some twelve households dispersed by NASS have moved back to London after suffering racial attacks.

Reception centres and large hotels

Large hostels and hotels may be particularly unsuitable for asylum-seeking children. They are institutional and no substitute for family housing. Yet much of the planned accommodation for NASS is in hostels and hotels, particularly in those offered by the private sector. Such accommodation also has a major effect on local primary schools and local GP surgeries. A small number of schools may receive a comparatively high number of asylum-seeking pupils who move on within a short time.

Social exclusion in London

An estimated 80 per cent of single adults and 50 per cent of families opted not be dispersed in the interim support system, or left their areas of dispersal within a few weeks of arrival. It is presumed that these families moved back to join compatriots in London and are likely to be living in overcrowded accommodation in the capital. This trend is likely to continue.

Lack of identified accommodation outside London

The whole future of the dispersal scheme still remains under question, as insufficient accommodation is being offered by the Regional Cluster Areas. The Home Secretary has the power to direct local authorities to take asylum-seekers but in doing this he is likely to cause major conflict with the receiving local authorities.

Refugee children's educational and social needs

As indicated above, poverty, poor housing, high mobility and a drop in social status are common experiences for asylum-seeking and refugee children. Other social and educational factors that affect significant groups of these children are:

- experiencing or witnessing war or other organised violence: for a small number this affects their ability to settle and to function in a new school in a new country

- living with families who do not know their educational and social rights

- having little access to early-years provision

- having had an interrupted education in their countries of origin

- being cared for by people other than their parents or usual carers

- speaking little or no English on arrival in Britain

- suffering bullying or isolation on arrival in school

Given these negative experiences, the following educational responses at an LEA, school and classroom level should be considered:

- Multi-agency working groups on refugees and asylum-seekers should be set up at local level where statutory sector agencies such as education, health, housing and social services meet with NGOs and plan services to refugees.

- A named person should be nominated within the LEA as having responsibility for refugees.

- Where there are large groupings of refugee children within the LEA, funding should be secured for a refugee support project. Such a project should act as a resource base and contact point within the LEA. The project should provide in-service training and should help schools develop their own practices, as well as supporting individual refugee children. Ideally the refugee support project should be multi-disciplinary, with staff input from the LEA psychological service, educational welfare service and the EAL team. Staff should also be employed with responsibility for home-school liaison, ideally with appropriate language skills.

- Schools should examine their induction policy and practices to provide a welcoming environment for refugee children (Bolloten and Spafford, 1998).

- School staff, in collaboration with other professionals, need to examine the support they give to refugee children who have had a traumatic past experience. Does a child need assessment and referral? Can school-based support be given? Does the child feel secure in school?

- A child's language needs should be met. Quality EAL support must be provided, ensuring that the curriculum is accessible. LEAs need to think about the language needs of children who have had no prior education before arriving in the UK. The school should encourage refugee students to develop their home languages.

- Schools should ensure that they have effective sanctions against those who bully refugees or subject them to racial harassment. Given the negative media coverage, schools should also use curricular and extra-curricular opportunities to make all pupils aware of refugee issues in a way that emotionally engages them and develops empathy.

- Refugees who arrive aged 14 or 15 years speaking little or no English need to have clear educational paths.

- Effective home-school liaison needs to be put in place.

- Refugee children need access to homework clubs and summer holiday projects, perhaps funded by the New Opportunities Fund (NOF), where their language and psychosocial needs can be met.

Good practice in all these areas currently exists, albeit patchily. For instance, many examples of good practice can be found among the LEAs that are operating refugee support projects (Rutter, 2001). At present some 32 local authorities have refugee support teachers or teams, some funded by EMAG, others directly by local authorities. The Refugee Council believes that the cost of meeting the additional educational needs of newly arrived refugee children will amount to £110-£120 per child per week. There are three possible ways of organising such support at an LEA level.

1. *The integrated refugee support team*, where all the additional educational needs of a refugee child are met within the team. Team members may include refugee support teachers whose job it is to provide EAL support and to organise any other support that child will need. Refugee support teachers may also act as a contact point within the LEA, organise in-service training and help schools develop their own practice. Educational welfare officers who assist with school admissions, home-school liaison staff and educational psychologists may also work in such an integrated refugee support team.

2. *A specialist refugee support teacher*(s) whose job is to work with refugee children whose needs go beyond the need to learn English: for example a child who is not coping as a result of an overwhelmingly traumatic past experience. The refugee support teacher may also act as a contact point within the local authority, run in-service training and help schools develop practices. The London Borough of Brent organises its work in this way.

3. No dedicated specialism by LEA staff, but *refugee children's needs met by EAL teachers*, the educational welfare officer, and so on.

Funding for refugee support work in education

Asylum-seeking children, like any other children, have their mainstream education funded through an annual allocation of monies from the DfEE. In England, local authorities and schools receive an allocation of funds based on pupil numbers on an annual census day (the Form Seven Census). For schools admitting large numbers of asylum-seeking pupils or other mobile groups, this annual census presents problems. A school may have no asylum-seekers on roll on the day of the census, but admit a number of such children a few weeks later. The school and the LEA will receive no funding for them until the following year.

However, LEAs and schools can access additional funding for specific projects to support refugee children – in their learning of English, for example. The support of refugee children in schools can be funded

• directly by a local authority

• by EMAG funds in England

• by other sources of funding such as the Single Regeneration Budget, Education Action Zones and the Excellence in Cities programme

Throughout the late 1980s and 1990s, the funding of specific refugee support work in education was a political issue. Until 1998, funding for refugee support in England and Wales came from Section 11 of the Local Government Act 1966 – a Home-Office-administered fund with 90 per cent of monies going to EAL support in schools. The aim of Section 11 was to make payment to local authorities to make special provisions for those whose 'language and customs differ from those of the community'. From 1966 to 1993 funding was limited to projects working with minority groups from Commonwealth countries.

Section 11 was a controversial source of funding, as Hugh South has discussed in Chapter 1. Educationalists and pressure groups from ethnic minority communities held different views on its value. Some argued that the motives behind Section 11 were assimilationist, while others argued that Section 11 marginalised EAL teaching because it was a special fund coming from the Home Office rather than from the DfEE. There were also concerns about its misuse: schools used Section-11-funded teachers to provide cover for absent staff or to teach mainstream subjects. It was these concerns about its misuse that prompted the Home Office to evaluate the use of Section 11 funds in 1988 (Home Office, 1989).

After this scrutiny report, greater emphasis was put on projects that were meant to improve the access to mainstream services. The scrutiny report demanded that projects had clear objectives, and the capacity to misuse the fund was diminished as projects were inspected and audited. Small amounts of Section 11 monies were made available to the voluntary sector as part of the Ethnic Minority Grant after the 1988 scrutiny report. Among refugee organisations this was mainly used to fund employment training projects.

However, Section 11 was still limited to projects working with ethnic minority populations from Commonwealth countries. But only 30 per cent of asylum-seekers arriving in 1993 came from Commonwealth countries. At a time of growing refugee arrivals (44,840 asylum applications in 1991, compared with 3,998 in 1989) this presented a real problem to local authorities in London (British Refugee Council, 1987). By 1993, some 15 London local authorities and the City of Manchester were educating more than 500 refugee children per LEA. The language support of 70 per cent of them could not legally be funded by Section 11 although some children did receive language support 'through the backdoor' using Section-11-funded staff.

In 1993, in response to lobbying from the Refugee Council, Neil Gerrard MP sponsored a Private Members Bill which aimed to extend provision to all 'ethnic minority communities whose language and customs differ from those of the rest of the community'. Home Office support was given to this amendment and the Local Government (Amendment) Act 1993 was passed. However, support for this measure was not unanimous, with opposition being voiced by organisations such as the Runneymede Trust, who saw the broadening of Section 11 as spreading scarce money even more thinly. During the passage of this Act, there was some extremely acrimonious debate, with the refugee lobby being pitted against organisations representing black and other ethnic minority communities.

But just as the Home Office extended the target groups for Section 11 funding, it cut the Section 11 budget and made some major administrative changes. A fund of £130.8 million in 1993/4 was cut to £110.7 million in 1994/5. The proportions of Section 11 paid by the Home Office was reduced from 75 per cent to about 57 per cent, placing further financial strain on LEAs. The jobs of many Section 11 teachers were threatened and many others were involved in campaigns to keep resources (Rutter, 1994). Many EAL teachers were left exhausted by campaigning.

In 1995/96 further changes were mooted, with the proposal to move some of Section 11 from the Home Office into a big new urban regeneration fund called the Single Regeneration Budget. The Refugee Council opposed this change: Section 11 projects were targeted at people, but the Single Regeneration Budget was targeted at an area. In consequence, it was feared that refugees would have to compete for funds against big, high-profile construction projects. However, this threat to Section 11 was not fully realised. In 1995, Section 11 continued to fund most school-based EAL projects in England and Wales. More specifically for refugee pupils, it funded ten of the fifteen LEA refugee support projects.[14] However, it did not fund LEA-based work that aimed to challenge racial harassment in schools. Nor was it available for home language teaching.

Further financial cuts were proposed in 1996, although never implemented as there was a change of government in 1997. Within six months, the Home Office had launched a major consultation exercise on the future of Section 11. It became clear that Section 11 as a Home-Office-administered fund was under threat.

In response to the Home Office consultation of 1997, the Refugee Council surveyed all EAL projects that worked with substantial numbers of refugee children. They presented to interested parties in local authorities four different options for funding projects to support refugee children (Refugee Council, 1998). These were:

1. status quo – Section 11 to remain within the Home Office

2. a broadened Section 11 fund to remain with the Home Office

3. transfer of Section 11 education monies to the DfEE.

4. transfer of Section 11 monies to the DfEE followed by greater delegation to schools.

Some 58 per cent of those surveyed favoured option two, with 31 per cent favouring a move to the DfEE. Following this consultation, Section 11 was moved to the DfEE and used to form the Ethnic Minority Achievement Grant (EMAG). This became EMTAG in 1999, when Traveller education monies were absorbed into the fund, and reverted to EMAG, in 2000.

From a refugee perspective, five main problems are associated with EMAG:

1. Funding has decreased at a time when the numbers of children requiring EAL support have increased. A Section 11 fund of £130.8 million in 1993/94 was cut to an EMAG fund of £83 million in 1998/99.

2. There is no contingency element in the EMAG grant. Local authorities have to make an annual bid for EMAG funds.

But the arrival of asylum-seeking children within a local authority is usually unpredictable, with many LEAs being unable to claim monies for children who arrive mid-way through a financial year. As asylum-seekers were dispersed outside London, many coastal and northern local authorities complained that they were not receiving additional monies to meet the needs of asylum-seeking students.

3. EMAG is reluctant to allocate grants for funding dedicated educational psychologists and educational social workers to support refugee children. Yet good practice indicates that multi-disciplinary teams are best able to meet the complex needs of refugee children

4. EMAG does not allow for the funding of home language teaching, even though this has educational and psychosocial benefits for refugee children. The DfEE policy is that home language teaching is the responsibility of the communities concerned

5. Non-governmental organisations are unable to access grants from EMAG.

As well as these problems and even more important, there has been no real national discussion of rights and entitlements to language support. Does thirteen days of in-class support or partnership teaching constitute sufficient support for a newly-arrived bilingual child who speaks little English? Is not this institutional racism, and would we tolerate such feeble support for other groups of children? There has been precious little open debate about this. Research carried out by the author indicates that there is a big variation in the amount of English language support bilingual children are given and also in the method by which this is delivered. For example, a child in one local authority may only receive in-class support for one day per week for one term. In a neighbouring local authority, children may receive all their in-class support from bilingual classroom assistants. In other schools, children who have achieved a greater level of English language fluency may be given some support.

The Refugee Council believes that the inconsistencies in the way in which language support is delivered, plus the lack of debate about how much EAL support a child should receive is caused by a lack of central government policy guidance on the rights of children from ethnic minority communities. A more children's-rights-focused approach is needed and the DfEE needs to be the lead agency in formulating such a national language strategy. Such a language strategy is essential if refugee children's educational needs are to be met. It is a major challenge for EMAG.

An invisible minority?
Turkish Cypriot educational
achievement

Crispin Jones

We owe the Turkish population the honour of knowing what is expected. (A headteacher interviewed during the research)

This chapter is based on a recent research study undertaken for the Turkish Cypriot Forum on the educational needs of Turkish Cypriot children.[15] The research revealed a complex and under-researched set of educational needs that teachers of such children need to be aware of if the group's educational achievement is to improve. Specifically, EMAG gives the opportunity for specialist and mainstream teachers to tackle the issue of Turkish Cypriot educational achievement in a more systematic and determined way. LEAs and schools with significant numbers of such children are now both aware of this issue and taking steps to improve their provision for this group. However, much remains to be done and there is a real need for dissemination of successful practice in this area. This chapter briefly reviews the main findings of the research and, as an appendix, gives a checklist, the work of Jim Wight, to help schools and LEAs improve the educational achievement of this currently under-achieving group of schoolchildren.

Turkish Cypriot underachievement in schools has a long history, a fact confirmed by this research. In looking at statistics from four London LEAs, it was clear that there was widespread low achievement, the Turkish-speaking communities being amongst the lowest achievers in all four LEAs at Key Stages 1, 2 and 3 as well as at GCSE. The collection of such statistics also revealed some interesting facts about the status of this community. Perhaps the most important of these is the need to make a distinction between Turkish Cypriots and other groups of Turkish-speaking children. (The research found that many schools still do not make distinctions between the various groups of Turkish-speaking children.) Where this distinction was made, Turkish Cypriot children still did poorly, performing below average in most LEA assessment categories. It should also be noted that in some cases, the LEAs themselves underperformed, making the underachievement of the Turkish Cypriot children extremely serious.[16] One of the few positive points to emerge from the data was that Turkish Cypriot girls were performing relatively well, often at or near national averages.

However, the general attainment levels need to be seen alongside evidence of a vibrant community, some of whose children achieve at the very highest level. Given this and also the fact that many of the children speak English fluently, something is happening to affect their performance. In addition, the research confirmed that the Turkish Cypriot and other Turkish-speaking communities are a significant but generally overlooked group in London schools. Their relative lack of educational success has long been recognised within the community and partially documented but, in the main, remains unaddressed by the education system as a whole.[17] Aydin Mehmet Ali, a leading researcher and writer on Turkish Cypriot education, calls this lack of attention 'invisibility' (Mehmet Ali, 1989, 1991, 1998). Some of the reasons for this include the fact that the group is small in size and thus is not often seen in official statistics; they are usually in small numbers in schools and are again likely to be overlooked; their culture, history and language are rarely known about and are seldom mentioned in classrooms.

The research made a series of concrete suggestions for improvement, addressed to both LEAs and schools. Jim Wight's list, appended to this chapter says much that is important but little that is new. This is because many of the causes of poor educational achievement are known. (It is interesting to compare this list with that presented by Peter Nathan as an appendix to Chapter 2.) What prevents improvement is not so much lack of knowledge as the pressures that are currently being put on all teachers. Perhaps more significant, as the work of David Gillborn and Deborah Youdell reveals (Gillborn and Youdell, 2000), is that the concentration on general system improvement works differentially. In other words, general system improvement has taken place but the gap between disadvantaged groups and the norm has widened rather than narrowed.

How it deals with such groups of school children who are systematically failed by the system could be a measure of the effectiveness of a national education system. The Turkish Cypriot community is well established but its relative educational failure continues to go unnoticed. Such research as has been done on this community is relatively small-scale, but when reviewed for the present study, some themes did come through clearly as being significant:

- Turkish Cypriot educational underachievement was identified nearly 30 years ago but remains an issue.

- Confusion remains about terminology and data collection.

- The complexity of language issues about the range and status of Turkish spoken in Britain, and the implications of this for education, remain relatively unexplored.

- School and community support for bilingualism is crucial to educational success.

- Racism is a factor but further research is needed to clarify its impact on the lives of Turkish Cypriot children.

- Gender differences in achievement remain but are constantly changing.

- Home-school-community relations were identified early as an issue and remain one.

- Lack of understanding of the educational system remains an issue that schools find difficult to address effectively (derived from ICIS, 1999).

Given this range of concerns, how is the education service dealing with them? In the ICIS research, a wide range of opinions was canvassed. However, in this brief chapter I wish to look at the expressed perspectives of teachers, headteachers and LEA officers, as they are among the key players in raising the achievement levels of Turkish Cypriot children.

The interviews gave a positive insight into schools' and teachers' understanding of, and effective dealing with, the issues raised by the presence of Turkish Cypriot children. Although worried by the lack of educational achievement of many of these children, all the teachers were keen to stress positive aspects and individual success stories. There was a widespread feeling that the parents were willing to help the school with their children's learning. School initiatives, for example in relation to home reading and homework generally, were seen as being supported by the Turkish Cypriot community, even if the level of support was uneven. The children too, especially at primary school level, were in general proud of their culture and eager to learn in the British school system. One teacher claimed that 'Turkish kids are desperate to show off their culture' and that this was 'a real opportunity we use but don't make the most of'. As with other pupils from minority groups, it was felt by almost all the teachers that the more use schools made of the pupils' own cultural knowledge and understanding, the more effective they became in raising educational standards and improving inter-group relations. Pupils whose background is given status in the school setting, it was argued, gain in confidence and ability to learn effectively.

A further factor was numbers: being seen by teachers and other pupils as a significant group within the school seemed to have a positive effect on Turkish Cypriot children's confidence. However, one head remarked that 'having significant numbers seems to be a virtue in relation to their confidence in school but we don't take advantage of it'.

Many teachers also saw the issue of bilingualism as a positive factor, although how far that approval was reflected in classroom practice was difficult to judge. They felt that Turkish-speaking children who were brought up in actively bilingual homes had a good chance of succeeding in school. As one said, it is 'a new world of languages which they can join' when they go to the English medium school as confident English and Turkish speakers – and this confidence, it was felt, had a beneficial effect throughout their schooling. There was no doubt however, that most of the teachers felt that fully functioning bilingual children do have an advantage in school and indeed, in later life.

A positive aspect that emerged from the research was that the teachers interviewed felt that there was little racism directed against these groups of children and that they did not seem to be victims of Islamaphobia. This was not a blindness to racism: they felt that other groups suffered far more in comparison. How far such relative weightings have value, however, is open to question.

Teachers were also concerned about why their practice was not being effective. EAL provision was constantly mentioned, particularly for children whose English was already at a reasonable level. Main-stream classroom teachers felt unconfident to supply effective advanced EAL support in their classrooms and their comments on outside EAL support (whether provided in school or by the LEA) was often less than flattering.

Many of the teachers also mentioned that their schools did not seem able to build on the Turkish Cypriot community parents' obvious enthusiasm for education. Two teachers coupled this view with the fact that many of the children seemed to have low self-esteem or low expectations about their ability to learn in school; one went on to say that this had to be an issue for the school as the children concerned appeared to be confident outside school. However, more teachers felt that this whole issue was tied up with the low expectations that many teachers had of Turkish-speaking children generally, especially if their EAL needs were very apparent. Again, this point reflected the confusion in schools about the various Turkish-speaking com-munities. Lumping them together is not helpful if targeted help is to be provided.

This low level of achievement, claimed the majority of the teachers interviewed, could be more effectively tackled if there was better communication between the school and the homes of the children, i.e. better home-school-community links. But many felt that although this was desirable, the work pressures placed on teachers by SATs, OFSTED, curriculum development and so on made progress in this important area unlikely. Some felt that stronger support from their LEA in this respect would be helpful, particularly in the area of practical help based on policy statements that took the issue of Turkish Cypriot pupil underachievement seriously. Also, for a few of the teachers, the main purpose of better home-school links seemed to be a one-way process of informing rather than learning from parents. When links with local supplementary schools were mentioned as a possible starting point, nearly all the teachers stated that although they were aware such schools existed and that a number of their pupils attended them, they had not had the time to make such links. The only teachers who had good knowledge of and strong links with such schools were the teachers who themselves came from the community concerned and who very often taught in such schools as well.

When asked what the schools could do better to meet the needs of such pupils, particularly in relation to supporting work funded by EMAG, a long list of initiatives was proposed. Amongst the more significant were:

- *More use of the Turkish language in the classroom.* Although most schools had some curriculum materials in Turkish, all the teachers said that there was a need for more Turkish-language curriculum materials in the schools and that more information in Turkish should be going home. There was approval for the greater use of Turkish in classrooms but widespread uncertainty about how this should be organised and utilised for learning.

- *Improving home-school relations.* Suggestions included having parents' rooms, strategies to help non-literate parents assist in their children's learning, looking at the timing of parents' evenings and perhaps having targeted parents' evenings in Turkish. And some said that more interpreters were needed.

- *Information for teachers.* It was felt that more needed to be known about the Turkish Cypriot community, particularly their recent history, their religion and their language. Some of the teachers were unclear about much of this and considered that their ignorance was widely shared by colleagues: it was not so much that teachers had stereotypes but rather that they knew very little about the community – a reference to the invisibility noted earlier in this chapter. This issue – invisibility – may also reflect the ambiguity about Turkish identity and culture within the British imagination. Much of the social construction of Europe over the last thousand years or so has arisen out of opposition to Islam and the Turkish/Ottoman empire: this is still not really taught in our schools so the teachers' information deficit is not surprising (Coulby and Jones, 1996).

Finally, when the teachers were asked to identify the single most important factor in raising Turkish Cypriot pupils' attainment, they offered a wide range of suggestions. What was interesting was that in nearly all cases, they considered that it was up to their school to take the initiative. Some teachers thought it was important for parents to help with homework but that it was up to the school to persuade them to do this and to advise them about how it might best be done. Others, as mentioned earlier, believed that more use should be made of Turkish in the school. Finally, some teachers felt that their school should take the initiative in supporting bilingualism in the home: they were not advocating transitional bilingualism but were committed to the belief that strong bilingualism is the key to success for this group of pupils.

In conclusion, the impression given by these concerned teachers was that while they were aware of underachievement, and also of some of the solutions for it, the pressures on their time made progress slow and difficult. The strongest impression that emerged was of a strong sense of commitment to raising the educational achievements of Turkish Cypriot children, coupled with puzzlement at the current low levels of achievement. Indeed, recognising and precisely identifying the issues involved in Turkish Cypriot achievement is a crucial first step in dealing with it.

Given the importance of the LEA for supporting EMAG work, it is necessary to know how LEA officers perceive the specific issue of Turkish Cypriot under-achievement. Talking to officers in LEAs with significant numbers of Turkish Cypriot children, it became clear that the underachievement of these pupils was a cause for concern and action. At the LEA level, as at the school level, specific policies were rare, because it was expected that policies relating to ethnic minorities, asylum-seekers, refugees and EAL learners would have a positive effect on these children. Within that broad context however, specific targeted policies, anticipating EMAG, were being undertaken. Examples included supporting local Turkish and Turkish Cypriot community groups and educational forums, producing booklets about the local Turkish community, providing interpretation services and ensuring that key educational documents, such as application forms for LEA grants and services and information leaflets, were produced in Turkish. Data collection was improving and, although not perfect, it was increasingly allowing the picture of Turkish Cypriot and other Turkish-speaking young people's underachievement to be seen more clearly. Perhaps most important of all, most officers felt that LEAs were well on the way to providing good EAL and other services to schools following the difficult transition from Section 11 to the new EMAG system of funding.

However, LEA officers, like teachers, acknowledged that, despite their efforts, little progress was being made. Part of the problem was the current maelstrom of work, with new initiatives, including OFSTED inspection, being required of inner-city LEAs. Many thought that equal-opportunities work generally, and intercultural education policy in particular, remain matters more of rhetoric than of reality, not only in the LEAs but also in the DfEE and OFSTED, despite the findings of Macpherson on the Stephen Lawrence murder inquiry. Given that the officers interviewed had job briefs which included some aspects of equal opportunities, such a perspective is perhaps inevitable in light of the competition for ever-shrinking LEA resources and increasing job insecurity in London's LEAs. In this context, it is hardly surprising that community education forums are not nurtured or strongly supported, that liaison projects fail to become embedded in school and LEA practice and that EAL support is patchy and uneven.

As well as delivering existing services more effectively to local communities and schools, the LEA officers saw scope for other activities that could help tackle underachievement:

- *Co-ordination.* LEAs needed to co-ordinate better, both internally and with other local services. This would clearly benefit Turkish Cypriot parents and their children. Co-ordination was also needed between the LEA, the Turkish Cypriot community and the schools. More generally, the LEA's monitoring and support role could help to ensure the more effective use of existing resources in schools to help pupils from Turkish-speaking communities, especially in relation to EAL, EMAG bids and general policies, practice and evaluation. (It is a hopeful sign that several of the LEAs involved in the research are now starting targeted programmes aimed at raising Turkish Cypriot achievement.)

- *Information.* Like the teachers interviewed, LEA officers felt that lack of information about the Turkish Cypriot, and indeed other Turkish-speaking, communities was widespread both in their LEA administration and in their schools. Such information could be provided alongside information about existing good practice. With growing Internet use this will be easier to do than in the past, as the national EAL e-mail list illustrates. The community also needed to be kept better informed about what was happening to their children in schools, and about their rights and responsibilities. This obviously had to be done in close co-operation with the schools.

Some LEA officers stated what was probably felt by all, namely that LEAs respond to pressure from community groups and tend to ignore them if they do not push. (The same is true in schools; pupils who underachieve and who are quiet are generally left alone.) When asked to name the most important single thing that could be done to enhance achievement of these pupils, two areas stood out: supporting literacy programmes for parents, and raising the status of EAL work by improving the quality of EAL staff.

Both groups, the teachers and the LEA officers, seemed aware of the issues facing Turkish Cypriot children. Many felt that they knew the strategies that would enhance performance and welcomed EMAG if it meant that specific resources and attention could be directed towards this group of school children. But they also realised that they were a thin sliver of margarine on a very large slice of bread. Spread too thinly, they felt they would be ineffective. Concentrating on some would be to the detriment of others. All felt that the level of resourcing, EMAG notwithstanding, was wholly inadequate.

The picture that the research revealed is thus a patchy one. The evidence of under-achievement is becoming clearer and better known as more accurate statistics are being collected at both LEA and school level. Awareness of the issue, as noted earlier, is the first concrete step in putting specific targeted programmes in place. Some of the LEAs and schools with significant numbers of Turkish Cypriot pupils are organising EMAG and other more broadly-based projects to help raise achievement. There is hope that these projects will at last begin improving the levels of Turkish Cypriot children's achievement significantly.

APPENDIX – *Jim Wight*
Proposals for action at classroom, school and LEA level to raise the achievement of Turkish Cypriot and other Turkish-speaking pupils

The following checklist was compiled by Jim Wight for the research project on which this chapter was based. It provides a framework for reviewing practice at classroom, school and LEA level and deciding priorities for action. Like many other such lists, the suggestions seem obvious but the practice proposed is often not followed in classrooms, schools and LEAs. Consequently, in section 6.11, it proposes robust monitoring and evaluation of the policies proposed, to ensure that they are firmly embedded in classroom, school and LEA practice.

1. Working with families
Classroom level

- Do parents feel that they have clear information about what their children are learning and how they are progressing?

- Are parents confident that they can raise questions or discuss concerns about their children's experience, achievements or difficulties in the classroom?

- Are there successful arrangements to encourage home-school partnership over particular learning objectives and activities (e.g. homework, attendance, etc.)?

School level

- Is there a clear, consistently applied school policy on communicating and working with parents?

- Are there arrangements to enable communication with families to take place using the language of the home where this is likely to be helpful?

- Are sufficient staff time and resources made available to develop and sustain productive partnerships between home and school?

LEA level

- Are there specific LEA facilities (such as translation services) or initiatives (such as action research projects) to improve schools' partnerships with parents/families?

2. Working with the community
Classroom level

- Are the staff well informed about the local Turkish-speaking communities and aware both of their diversity and the things they have in common?

- Are staff aware and supportive of pupils' links with local community organisations (such as language or supplementary classes)?

School level

- Has the school established a dialogue and ways of collaborating with the Turkish-speaking communities locally?

- Are the Turkish-speaking communities represented on or in productive contact with the school's governing body?

LEA level

- Has the LEA established procedures for consulting with Turkish-speaking communities locally?

- Has the LEA identified areas for joint projects or other forms of collaboration with Turkish-speaking communities?

3. Receiving newcomers
Classroom level

- Are there established strategies for making new class members welcome and accepted into the peer group (such as the 'buddy' system)?

- Are there established strategies for helping new arrivals (especially those with little experience of English) to understand classroom activities and their role in the classroom?

School level

- Are there effective induction procedures for new pupils to the school, especially those who are new to English and/or refugees from conflict areas?

- How does the school ensure that key information about new pupils is collected, communicated to and used constructively by relevant members of staff?

LEA level

- How does the LEA maintain an overview of the pattern of new arrivals such as refugees and the implications for school admissions and resourcing policies?

4. Raising expectations

Classroom level

- Are there opportunities for staff to focus on the vital role of expectations in the classroom and their impact on pupils' achievement? In particular:

    - how pupils' expectations and belief in their own ability as learners affect their achievement

    - how teachers' expectations influence pupils' views of their own potential

    - how pupils form their views about teacher expectations of them

    - how teachers can balance their concern not to discourage pupils by setting tasks that are too hard for them with the goal of establishing high expectations for future achievement.

School level

- How does the school use target-setting to raise the expectations and achievements of individuals and groups?

- Does the school have specific targets for raising the achievement of Turkish-speaking pupils?

- Does the school have strategies for identifying and addressing underachievement across the range of pupil performance?

LEA level

- Does the LEA's EMA action plan have specific targets for raising the achievement of Turkish-speaking pupils?

- How does the LEA ensure that all schools with Turkish-speaking pupils, especially those with small numbers, share the LEA focus on raising their achievement?

5. Tackling racism
Classroom level

- Does the ethos of the classroom clearly value ethnic diversity and challenge racist perceptions?

- Is there a good understanding of how different groups of ethnic minority pupils, including Turkish-speaking pupils, experience and perceive racism?

- Is there an understanding of how pupils experience low expectations of them in school as an aspect of racism?

School level

- Has the school developed a shared understanding of both overt and unintentional racism and strategies for addressing it?

- Has the school developed effective strategies to address bullying?

LEA level

- How do LEA antiracist and equal opportunities policies support progress in schools in tackling racism?

6. Extending language skills
Classroom level

- Are the staff aware of the language repertoires of the pupils they are working with?

- Do Turkish-speaking and other bilingual pupils have their home languages acknowledged, valued and given a role in the classroom?

- Are all staff confident about their roles in helping to extend pupils' language and communication skills?

School level

- Is there a satisfactory school system for identifying pupils who need help with learning English, and for providing this help?

- Does the school encourage Turkish-speaking and other bilingual children to become literate and to gain qualifications in their home languages?

LEA level

- Does the LEA have a flexible system for ensuring that appropriate levels of funding are allocated to schools to meet the identified needs of bilingual and other minority pupils?

- Does the LEA have a strategy to encourage and facilitate opportunities for Turkish-speaking and other bilingual pupils to sustain and develop their home language skills?

- Does the LEA have ways of identifying common issues or concerns in schools about their language-development policies and practices and of initiating inservice training or action research to address these concerns?

7. Improving access to learning
Classroom level

- Are staff confident in using a range of classroom strategies to ensure that EAL pupils, pupils with literacy difficulties and those underachieving for other reasons have regular access to appropriate and challenging learning activities?

- In particular, are staff well versed in approaches that capitalise on children's interests and strengths (e.g. the home languages of English beginners, the oral skills of poor readers and writers) and do they provide support to over-come areas of weakness (e.g. opportunities for additional practice, peer group activities and support, specially focused homework tasks)?

School level
- Are there procedures to promote the sharing of the most effective classroom practice and to enable joint problem-solving activity when staff identify individuals or groups that are not engaging successfully in curriculum activities?

LEA level
- Does the LEA identify best practice in inclusive education and promote it through INSET strategy, curriculum development activities and other forms of guidance?

8. Using additional teaching support effectively
Classroom level
- Are staff whose role is to provide specialist teaching support for EAL learners and those with other learning needs de-ployed effectively?

- When specialist support staff work in partnership with class or subject teachers are their reciprocal roles and respon-sibilities clearly established (e.g. lesson preparation, class-room management, marking, etc.)?

School level
- Do school policies on teaching and learning recognise the role of teaching partnerships in developing and disseminat-ing more effective classroom practice?

- Does school practice in timetabling and staff deployment support the development of effective teaching partnerships?

LEA level

- How does the LEA seek to ensure that EAL teachers and other specialist support staff are professionally well equipped in their teaching and partnership roles?

9. Responding to Turkish perspectives

Classroom level

- Are there opportunities for Turkish-speaking pupils, along with those of other ethnic backgrounds to share experiences, concerns and views and to affirm their cultural identity?

- Does the curriculum positively reflect the nature of multi-cultural society and, in particular, present an informed picture of the culture and heritage of Turkish-speaking communities?

- Are pupils, especially those identified as underachieving, invited to give their analysis of how they could be helped to learn more successfully and to improve their achievement in school?

School level

- Are members of Turkish-speaking and other ethnic minority communities appropriately represented on the school staff?

- Has the particular contribution these staff can make to the school (in addition to their general responsibilities) because of their linguistic skills and cultural perspectives been explored, agreed and supported?

LEA level

- Does the LEA have strategies to ensure that Turkish-speaking and other ethnic minority staff are appropriately represented and that their insights are taken into account in schools and other educational services?

10. Monitoring achievement and evaluating progress
Classroom level

- Do staff consistently monitor the progress of pupils they are working with and use the information to identify and provide more effectively for individual pupils who are underachieving?

School level

- Does the school analyse information collected on pupils' achievement to monitor the progress of all Turkish-speaking pupils, including those receiving EAL support, and use this analysis to provide more effective strategic support where there is evidence of underachievement?

- Does the school monitor and evaluate how policies and initiatives designed to address pupils' underachievement are being implemented across the school?

LEA level

- Does the LEA system for monitoring ethnic minority pupils' achievement provide specific information on the achievement of Turkish-speaking pupils and allow for comparisons to be made between:

  - Turkish Cypriot and Turkish mainland communities?

  - relatively recent arrivals (including refugees) and pupils who are second- or third-generation members of their communities?

- Does the LEA have effective ways to monitor and evaluate how key elements in their EMA action plan (including those relating to Turkish-speaking pupils) are being implemented in schools?

5

Specialist support for Gypsy Traveller children in primary and secondary schools

Kalwant Bhopal

Traveller Children were included in the EMTAG grants for 1999 and 2000, so have become the concern of EMAS across Britain. Accordingly, we include this chapter here.

This chapter explores specialist support for Gypsy Traveller children in primary and secondary schools in the UK.[19] It examines the value of the specialist support measures adopted by Traveller Education Services (TESs) in schools which facilitate and promote regular attendance; these include transport arrangements, the provision of uniforms and liaison with the Education Welfare Service (EWS). It also explores how learning is supported through study and homework support and the designation of sanctuary territory. Such specialist support in schools is crucial in encouraging successful attendance, access to curriculum and satisfactory achievement levels for Gypsy Traveller children. It is also an essential prerequisite for effective work with this group of generally socially excluded children.

The poor participation and low levels of achievement in education by Gypsy Traveller children have been known for a long time (Central Advisory Council for Education, 1967; Reiss, 1975; Worrall, 1979; DES, 1983, 1985). Recent research (OFSTED, 1996, 1999) has detailed 'good practice' in schools, but still expressed serious concerns about access, attendance and achievement for Gypsy Traveller children. Blair and Bourne (1999) highlighted similar concerns, but emphasised the need for further detailed research in this area of education. Recent evidence on the education of Gypsy Travellers was published by OFSTED in March 1999 (OFSTED, 1999). One of the main conclusions the report emphasised was that:

> Gypsy Traveller pupils are the group most at risk in the education system; although some make a reasonably promising start in primary school, by the time they reach secondary level their generally low attainment is a matter of serious concern. (OFSTED, 1999, p. 11)

This view is supported by Kiddle (1999), who provides an insightful analysis of the changing relationship between Gypsy Travellers and schools and the impact this has had on both cultures. She also outlines the difficulties for Gypsy Travellers of gaining a successful education, as well as the role of the school in being responsive to Gypsy Traveller children's needs. These findings were supported by research carried out by the Essex Travellers Education Service (Essex TES, 1997) on the views of secondary-age Gypsy Traveller children and their parents. This research also demonstrated the need for all personnel in schools to be actively involved in encouraging and engaging their Gypsy Traveller pupils.

> Good practice in the schools was evident when the whole school ethos embodied *a will to educate all pupils* [original emphasis], including short-stay Travelling pupils, taking fully into account individual cultural, social and academic needs... Most success is achieved where the particular needs of Traveller children have been discussed, understood and accepted by the staff as a whole, through the leadership of key personnel. (Essex TES, 1997, p. 10)

The research also found that parents and young children expressed concerns about the social environment of secondary schools and described their fear of losing their cultural identity when attending secondary schools.

In seeking to resolve these issues, Heighway and Moxham (1998) identified the barriers in schools and the education system which may prevent Gypsy Traveller children from achieving. These included lack of positive perceptions of Traveller pupils; adapt the curriculum to the needs of Traveller pupils, provision of vocational courses; refusal to admit cultural diversity, and lack of resources relevant to Traveller pupils and of materials for teachers on tackling discrimination.

Recent research into successful practice in the education of Gypsy Traveller children (Bhopal *et al.* 2000) demonstrates that the issues of low attendance, access to curriculum and achievement levels of such children can be successfully addressed by schools, LEAs and TESs.[20] Schools themselves have a crucial role to play in this. Factors that help include:

- having effective equal-opportunities policies that specifically mention Gypsy Traveller children and their needs

- constant monitoring and evaluation of such policies

- the importance of raising teacher expectations about Gypsy Travellers

- curriculum reviews to ensure that the Gypsy Traveller contribution to British society is acknowledged

- a pastoral care programme that is sensitive to the special needs of Gypsy Traveller children

- effective anti-bullying strategies

Some of the factors mentioned in relation to TESs include

- the importance of supportive advocacy for their clients

- effective INSET (In Service Education and Training)

- securing appropriate school places for Gypsy Traveller children

- facilitating and supporting learning by providing appropriate curriculum materials

- supporting the continuity of the educational experience of Gypsy Traveller children

The rest of the chapter looks at the findings of this research in more detail in the hope that they can help to improve the achievement levels of Gypsy Traveller children, the more so as such work can now be clearly targeted through the EMTAG and, since late 2000, specific grant.

The research was funded by the DfEE and the main aims of the project were to address issues of low attendance and achievement for Gypsy Traveller pupils in a number of primary and secondary schools.[21] Particular emphasis was placed on examining some of the contributory factors associated with poor attendance and under-achievement of Gypsy Travellers in schools; 'good practice' needed to be identified and used by other schools to improve matters.

The pupils included in this research mainly belong to semi-nomadic communities who live on official public or private caravan and mobile home sites. Though most of these families only travel for limited periods each year, some are more routinely nomadic and some of these suffer owing to the national lack of official sites. In consequence, some children may have limited educational opportunities, as frequent changes of school may affect their level of achievement.

The report found that the range of successful specialist support measures adopted by TESs in schools included facilitating and promoting regular attendance during the period immediately after admission, including

- organising transport arrangements

- help with the provision of uniforms

- effective liaison with the Education Welfare Seervice

- facilitating and supporting learning through appropriate curriculum materials and supporting the continuity of the children's educational experience

Facilitating and promoting regular attendance

TESs facilitated and promoted regular attendance in a number of ways in all the schools researched. Factors addressed related to:

Transport arrangements

All the TESs studied here were able to make transport a
for taking Gypsy Traveller pupils to and from school.
contracted taxi services: this was seen to be the most reliable and
cost-effective option. For many parents, the transport arrangements
were vital to get their children to attend school. Parents also felt that
taxis were safer for their children than travelling on public buses.
'The transport is important for us to get our kids to schools. If we
didn't have it, then they wouldn't go. And I know my kids are getting
there safely by car and not going on buses' (Gypsy Traveller parent).

The use of taxis, and in some cases school buses, is known to have
a significant impact on school attendance. The provision of transport
from home provides a daily structure and routine which is an important reassurance for the parents.

Provision of uniforms

A number of schools had access to uniform grants for Gypsy
Travellers, through the LEA or through the TES's specific uniform
budget. Those who did not, however, did not let this affect attendance. Many offered second-hand uniforms or provided new uniforms funded from the school's own resources. By providing
uniforms the TES was able to work with the school in identifying
and solving problems that can hinder or prevent regular attendance.
Many of the teachers felt that wearing a uniform affected whether or
not the child was accepted.

> We don't have a pupil uniform grant, but we work with the school to
> sell second-hand uniforms and to get Gypsy Traveller children to wear
> them. It makes a difference if the children are in uniform, because they
> feel they are part of the school and other children and the teachers
> accept them as being part of the school. (TES support teacher in
> secondary school)

In one of the case study schools, if the Gypsy Traveller pupils did not
have uniforms or PE kits, the TES teacher or the school often provided them. This approach indicated that Gypsy Traveller pupils
were visually included in the school; it was aimed at securing access
and equality of treatment for Gypsy Traveller pupils.

> If we know that some of the families don't have much money, we just help them out. If they need a new uniform and we can provide it, we'll do it. We want them to be the same as the other children and have what they have when they come to school. (classroom teacher in secondary school)

For these schools, the requirement of school uniform is not seen as a hindrance to admission or attendance. Any difficulties are appreciated and dealt with sensitively. If uniform is a prerequisite for obtaining access and attendance, then the school or the TES will make every effort to provide it.

Liaison with the Education Welfare Service

In all but one of the schools, the liaison with the specialist Education Welfare Officer (EWO) attached to the TES was very effective and productive in initiating and maintaining links with parents and the school, as well as in securing access and promoting levels of attendance. In one of the primary schools, the relationship between the specialist EWO and the school was crucial in monitoring and maintaining satisfactory attendance for Gypsy Traveller pupils.

> The EWO we have is very persistent at working with the families and the children, she does not let them go and keeps going back to make sure they are attending. She will also do what she has to do if they don't attend. (Headteacher in primary school)

The work of the EWO attached to the TES is primarily concerned with initiating contact with Gypsy Traveller families, developing positive relationships, securing school places and organising and encouraging regular attendance. It was effective in improving attendance, particularly for secondary-age children. In one school, incentives to encourage Gypsy Traveller children to attend included giving them book tokens to reward them for a full week's attendance at school. In another, regular attendance was supported by visiting parents regularly.

Supporting learning
Study and homework support

A number of the schools provided after-school support clubs where children were able to go for study support and help with other problems. In the research, it was the TES support teacher who provided the Gypsy Traveller pupils with this help. In some cases, for instance where the Gypsy Traveller pupil may have missed a deadline for coursework, the teacher was able to organise a planned programme of study for the pupil as well as to renegotiate deadlines. Such difficulties are often due to intermittent attendance caused by the travelling pattern of the families.

> I know that A won't be able to meet her deadline for her project and so she can come and see me and I can help her. I can help her with how to organise her work and if I have to, can go and see the teacher concerned. (Traveller teacher in secondary school)

Learning support in both primary and secondary schools included an early identification of any special educational needs and the provision of appropriate support within the limits of available resources. Some of the Gypsy Traveller pupils in the case study schools showed a weakness in language skills. In these cases, efforts were taken early to provide remedial support. In one of the primary schools, children in these circumstances were given extra time after school to catch up. They were supported in their numeracy and literacy needs by committed staff who were willing to stay on after school. In one of the secondary schools, it was recognised that some children needed support at home as well as at school. A number of children were lent laptop computers for them to use at home.

> Gypsy Traveller children aren't surrounded by books and computers like most children are nowadays. So they may be at a disadvantage when they're doing their homework. So we have some laptops that we have lent them and for some of the children this has made such a difference to their learning. (Traveller support teacher in secondary school)

The schools visited were aware of the difficulties that existed for some Gypsy Traveller children in relation to homework. Not all the children had a quiet space in which to do their homework or the materials they required. But the schools studied were supportive in helping children to complete their homework. One of the secondary schools regularly ran homework and breakfast clubs. Another had a Gypsy Traveller youth group. In addition to providing for the social needs of the pupils, the aim of the group was to offer recreational activities and to support their academic work. This group has been extremely successful with Gypsy Traveller pupils.

> Because this group exists for the Gypsy Traveller pupils, their self-esteem has been raised and they enjoy it. As a result the parents are able to trust their children to participate in out-of-school activities that otherwise they might not have done. (Traveller teacher)

The LEA Community Education staff who helped set up the Group have produced a book about Travellers, in collaboration with the TES, for children and staff. The book, aimed at removing some of the stereotypes that exist about Gypsy Travellers, has been well received by the Gypsy Traveller community and the school, and has also been popular with other agencies. Such practice demonstrates raising awareness of Gypsy Travellers in a positive way, and helps to promote trust and cement supportive relationships between Gypsy Traveller parents, pupils, staff and other agencies.

In the same school, the SEN department ran an English workshop once a week, which many Gypsy Traveller children attended. The main activities of the workshop included encouraging children to read, improving their writing and punctuation skills and raising their reading standards by exploring different types of books at appropriate reading levels. Such practice facilitates and aids access to the curriculum for Gypsy Traveller pupils as well as increasing individual motivation and achievement.

Designation of sanctuary territory
In all the schools, there was a special room or place where the Gypsy Traveller children could go if they had problems, or if they just wanted to feel they were in a safe place. Having a 'named person' and a 'place of safety' to which they can go helps the Gypsy Traveller pupils to become more confident about attending school and seeking advice and support concerning any difficulties they may be experiencing.

> The Gypsy Traveller children know they can come to me or they can go to the room where I am and sit in there. If they feel scared or if they have been bullied they can sit in there and feel safe and know that I will be there for them and help to sort things out for them. (Traveller teacher, primary school)

Having a 'named person' in an institution is an important point of contact for Gypsy Traveller pupils. Such sensitive provision can enhance the confidence pupils and parents have in the school and the staff.

> I know that if my son has a problem, he can always go to Mrs X (Traveller teacher) and she will listen to him and see what he has to say. He can always go and sit with her in her room and he tells me that this is a good thing. If it wasn't for her, I don't think my kids would go to school and they would have a harder time (Gypsy Traveller parent).

This chapter has sought to demonstrate how specialist support for Gypsy Traveller children in primary and secondary schools is vital in improving levels of achievement and attendance, as well as access. Such support measures are provided by the TESs, EWS and schools. When such inter-agency support is exercised, Gypsy Traveller children benefit. Support measures such as transport arrangements, the provision of uniforms and liaison with the EWS help to promote regular attendance. Study and homework support and the designation of sanctuary territory support the learning process itself. Such measures have to have the support of all personnel in order for them to be effective. It is hoped that these findings will help support work in relation to Gypsy Travellers in other schools.

Acknowledgements

I would like to thank the DfEE who provided funding to carry out the research. The views expressed in this article are the views of the author and not those of the Department. I would like to thank the staff of the six schools and TESs who participated in the research; they all gave their time generously and made me feel very welcome. I would also like to express my thanks to all the families who participated in the research, welcomed me into their homes and spoke openly about issues concerning them. I would finally like to thank Jagdish Gundara, Arthur Ivatts, Crispin Jones and Charlie Owen, who were part of the research team and read earlier drafts of this chapter and provided helpful comments.

6

Teachers talking: communication in professional partnerships

Angela Creese

Introduction

Schools now have greater freedom to determine how they spend money allocated through the Ethnic Minority Achievement Grant (EMAG) (DfEE, 1998b). How this affects resource decisions is still uncertain but it is likely that staffing will be targeted under the newly devolved funding arrangements. The time is ripe therefore to revisit the possibilities of partnership teaching (Bourne, 1989; Creese, 1997; Levine, 1990).

It may be useful to define 'partnership teaching'. Indeed much energy has gone into defining this concept and its ugly sisters 'support' and 'withdrawal'. Centred in a discourse of (teacher) persuasion, idealised descriptions of partnership teaching speak of teachers having equal status with shared responsibilities. Two teachers plan the curriculum and teaching strategies together, taking into account the needs of all the children in the class. In class they take it in turns to lead the lesson. Ultimately, this is a mutually beneficial and developmental relationship, with each teacher learning from the other (Bourne and McPake, 1991; Levine, 1990). Definitions of support modes of teaching on the other hand see the language support teacher working with a targeted child or children in a lesson in which the curriculum is planned and delivered by the subject teacher.

The terms 'support' and 'partnership' do little to get at the complexities of the professional relationship that teachers form with one another. It is rare to find a full, straightforward partnership. It is much more common to find language specialists in multiple relationships, each with differing levels of commitment. Teachers are not always able to form full partnerships with all their colleagues for a number of reasons: there may be resistance, there may be a lack of confidence, there may be a lack of management support, there may be a school ethos which creates a culture of isolation and competition rather than collaboration. Consequently, in any one school, a language specialist may work in a partnership with one teacher, in a support mode with another and may choose to withdraw students while working with another. Here it is important to recognise that withdrawal too is a mode of collaboration if it is done successfully. Teachers need to keep one another well informed if a child is taken out to work on supplementary aims.

Teachers and schools are much more likely to operate all three modes of inter-professional relationship than just one. But this does not support the argument which would lead us towards the conclusion that all modes are equal but different. I would take the opposite view. My argument is that each mode of teacher organisation comes already saturated with relations of power. My intention is to show that the way teachers organise their inter-professional teaching relationships, the roles and activities they play and, perhaps most importantly, the way they talk within these roles, maintains and creates power relations within the school which impact on how language, diversity, identity and learning are viewed. Teachers' inter-professional relationships are important because upon them hangs the infrastructure for the successful implementation of policies of educational inclusion for bilingual students.

My view is that language work in schools must move beyond a deficit position of support work for seemingly more important curriculum aims. Lest we forget, acquiring new knowledge is only one of the many functions that language manages in social life. Moreover, the learning of subject knowledge is only one of the many educational aims behind public schooling. We need to expand our knowledge and practice of what language work means in schools to include issues of social/cultural/linguistic identity, language and power, and the learning and maintenance of first and developing languages – a view of language work which sees it as more than a tool for curriculum learning. The introduction of EMAG is an appropriate time to rethink current approaches to EAL and to reconceptualise the language and mainstream debate (Leung *et al*, 1998; Tosi and Leung, 1999).

My contribution to this debate is to look at how teachers' interactions in different kinds of inter-professional relationships construct 'discipline specific' and 'language support' power relations and tensions in schools. The analysis that follows was drawn from research in three large secondary schools in multilingual and poor urban areas of inner and outer London.[22] I observed, interviewed and recorded in the classroom twenty-six teachers at work, twelve of whom were language specialists, the remainder subject specialists. Interestingly, only three of the twelve language specialists in the larger study described any of the work they did as partnership teaching: the majority spoke of their work as language and learning support.

In what follows, using the data collected during the research, I show that *partnership* relationships have some success in keeping language and diversity at the centre of the school's agenda while maintaining discourses of inclusion and respect for difference in classrooms. Teachers' talk, activities and roles in *support* relationships, on the other hand, tend to push language issues towards the periphery of classroom and school concerns. In the next section I look at some of the discourses which demarcate the two modes of teacher collaboration.

Participants and pedagogies: discourses of equality and hierarchy

Support work in the three schools was construed by subject specialists and students as being less important than the teaching of the curriculum subject. Knowledge and pedagogies were placed in an order of importance by participants, with language work falling behind curriculum work.

Extract One: *technology teacher, year 10*

> I mean standing up in front of twenty to thirty children, delivering and teaching, is a very arduous job. I think you just have to see support teaching as a different job. I think their role is totally different. They can work with a few kids who have special needs and problems and they can sort those through, which is not the same as teaching thirty children *en masse* hour after hour after hour. I mean that has got its demands. And it is not the same, it is a different job altogether. They get the same wage structure and things like that which perhaps they shouldn't, perhaps they should be seen as a separate entity, with different wage structures, different scales and things like that.

For this teacher, the 'arduous' work was delivering the curriculum to the many. Individual or small group teaching was associated with solving problems, not with knowledge expertise. This same teacher had a view of what counts as important knowledge:

Extract Two: *technology teacher, year 10*

> If it is technical language, I think it comes down to me, like technical words, like designing briefs, like ergonomics and things, but often the basic language and the simplification of language is done by the support teacher.

This teacher's language reconstituted already established hierarchies of expertise and pedagogies in education (Gee, 1999; Billig,1988). Expertise in a subject area has long been viewed by some as more important than the pedagogies necessary to deliver it effectively. Facilitation, scaffolding and 'simplifying' are likewise seen as skills that most have (for a discussion of this in terms of gender, see Creese and Hey, forthcoming). The teacher in Extract Two presented his responsibility for the technical language as specialised and contextualised knowledge whereas he saw the language specialist's responsibility for 'basic' language and the simplification of subject content as autonomous and generic knowledge (Lee, 1997, p. 76). Language specialists were seen as less knowledgeable about 'knowledges' which count. Their knowledge became unskilled knowledge – the beta to the subject specialists' alpha (Lee, 1997). Students too were able to read these signs:

Extract Three: *S = student, T = subject teacher*

S   But you're the proper teacher aren't you?

T   Well no. We are both proper teachers.

S   She's like a help

T   No, that's not true

In these extracts, an additional hierarchy was being constructed, this time around pedagogies. Subject teachers described their own role as 'explaining, instructing, directing' and the role of language specialists as 'accessing, simplifying, reworking, adapting'. This latter set of skills may be equally important to the bilingual learner in meeting their learning needs, but delivered in the mainstream classroom they are seen as skills with which the subject specialist is less involved and therefore as of secondary importance to the skills used for delivering the curriculum. Pedagogies associated with delivering subject expertise continue to take priority over discourses of learning which stress dialogue and facilitative talk. Thus, despite a huge literature on the importance of socio-cultural and dialogic approaches to learning (stemming from Vygotsky, 1986) and a second-language literature which stresses the importance of consciousness and awareness in language learning (Gass, *et al,* 1998; Harley, 1993, 1995; Long *et al,* 1983; Pica, 1991, 1995; Schmidt, 1990; Swain, 1985) there continues to be little opportunity in mainstream classrooms to use tasks and pedagogies which promote such language-learning opportunities.

Discourses of 'support' assist in the devaluation of these language-learning pedagogies in mainstream classrooms. Ironically, in restricting language work to learning work, a deficit view of language is left to fester: language must doggedly chase the tail of curriculum before learning is perceived to take place. Rather than making the most of diversity and difference, language continues to be regarded as a problem which impedes curriculum-learning aims. It is only when teachers work in partnership that some success is achieved in making language issues a central concern for the whole class. Subject and language teachers working in partnership see language learning and language for learning as parts of their joint responsibility. Moreover, views of language are extended beyond its referential and learning function to include its function in the construction of identity and its importance as linguistic and semiotic capital.

Extract Four: a) subject teacher – maths

I think because of my own background [Black male, South African, multilingual], I feel quite at ease and I will always. Even when a language support teacher is at a table with four children I will always go up and sit next to them or just eavesdrop, attending to facial expressions, even if I don't understand what is happening. You know, I just want to be part of that.

b) subject teacher – technology

I think it (language instruction) should be joint. I think I should get involved in language instruction as well. Perhaps because I taught English as a foreign language and am bilingual I do know some of the pitfalls. I have lived in countries where I can't speak the language and I know the situation, what it's like to be in a room when someone is giving a lecture and you don't understand much of what they are saying.

Partnerships allowed like-minded teachers to create a classroom culture more likely to see language and diversity as resources for learning than as obstacles to learning (Ruiz, 1984). A consideration of the importance of language in establishing social and cultural identity, as well as in its role as a teaching and learning tool, created a classroom culture which helped to construct this diversity as usual rather than problematic. Rather than viewing differences as restrictive in pursuing curriculum goals, they were viewed as a valuable resource in building knowledge in the classroom (Scardamalia and Bereiter, 1999). Language specialists in partnership had a position in mainstream education which support teachers were rarely accorded.

This section has looked at how educational discourses position language specialists who work in support and partnership modes of collaboration. I have tried to show that support modes of collaboration, however useful the pedagogic tools they draw upon, are not given equal status to that of their subject specialist colleagues. Schools, teachers themselves and students continue to see language issues in mainstream schools as less important than curriculum aims. We now turn to the communicative practices of the teachers themselves, to investigate how they maintain or transform these educational discourses in schools. In the following section, I look at how language specialists and subject specialists speak to the whole class. Differences in the way teachers used language to teach helped to reinforce their positions within the school as central or peripheral to educational debates and concerns.

Practice and power: core and peripheral curriculums

Sinclair and Coulthard's work on the regularity of teacher's discursive moves in whole-class teaching situations is well known (Sinclair and Coulthard, 1975). The initiation, response, feedback (IRF) sequence is a well-rehearsed routine in many educational settings. The ability to work with or against this class-fronted ritual is part of a teacher's definition. It is partly for this reason that the front of the class is such a powerful space. It is a place where teaching is perhaps at its most hierarchical. Here the teacher can explain, summarise, judge, give feedback, praise, condone and set future tasks. It is also, however, a highly risky space with real possibilities for a fall from grace. In this *performative* area, a teacher can be challenged, get things 'wrong' and lose face. Despite these risks it is a place that teachers usually stake out rather than avoid completely, although many teachers play down the hierarchy of the position. In my larger study (Creese, 1997), language specialists in support modes rarely took the front of the class and, when they did, it was for reasons other than direct subject teaching, usually as an auxiliary to it. Language specialists in teaching partnerships, however, were more likely to take up this position for both subject teaching and language work.

I found evidence of a classroom discursive formula being used by teachers when addressing the whole class. This consisted of a three-part functional move in which teachers directed students to do something. Put in more formal linguistic terms, the addresser, namely the teacher, used the 'emotive' function centred in the first-person pronoun 'I' to identify with, and constitute the importance of, what was being spoken about. By placing themselves at the centre of the speech situation, teachers could use the 'conative' function centred in the imperative and 'you' to tell the addressee, namely the student, to act. The student was asked to act upon the context in some way and in doing so, the 'referential' function, which is used to refer to and/or predict something in the context, was foregrounded (Jakobson, 1960, 1971, 1975). This three-part functional move, which I will refer to as IYS (**I** want **You** to do **Something**) was a re-curring move in the class-fronted teaching of secondary school classrooms. Of particular interest was the evidence I found which showed the subject and language specialists using IYS it differently. In the four subject-teacher extracts below, we can see the teachers using *'I'*, *'you'*, *'do something'* to make a claim on the students' actions through the completion of a teacher-owned task.

Extract Five: *a) humanities teacher – history*
> I want you to look for three things. I want you to look for the groups of people involved. I want you to look for the tools used and I want you to look for the result.

b) technology teacher 1
> Now I want to see copies of those things. And I want to see one in your file and one in your ID folder, all right?

c) technology teacher 2
> And I want you during the day, today, to think up a design for use yourself, not the group.

d) humanities teacher – geography
> What I want you to do is make sure you have your contents pages organised. I am going to give you until the last day of term to get your work completed.

This combination of language functions linked to a syntactic pattern places the subject teacher as the agent and self-nominated controller of classroom themes and action. Subject teachers use this formula to direct students to core curriculum concerns. There were fewer instances of language specialists using this formula, given that lan-guage specialists took the front of the class less often. On the rare occasions which they did, language and subject teachers were usually working together in partnership. Thus language specialists in partnerships were able to direct whole-class teaching and bring about student action in ways similar to subject specialists. In contrast, language specialists in support mode rarely used the combination of emotive, conative and referential functions in order to bring about student action. They did of course use 'I', but in ways which articulated peripheral curriculum concerns. One example of this is given below. The teacher uses 'I' not to set students tasks and control themes and events in the here and now but to define his usefulness for the students in the indefinite future. He sets out to explain to students how he might help them.

Extract Six: *language specialist in technology class*

(Subject teacher has just left the classroom for a couple of minutes.) Right, right. I won't waste everybody's time doing that now. What I am going to do when Miss Robins comes back – she is bringing a project on advertising which was done last year in order to show you – What I am going to do is type up for each of you a card, you know a piece of thin card, hole punched so that you can keep it in – Nihan, please don't talk while I am doing this otherwise we won't understand – and I will list all the homeworks week by week for this project, so that way if you miss one because you were absent or for whatever reason, you will have a total record of what the homeworks are.

What is interesting in this extract is the missing conative function. There is no mention of 'you' (i.e. the student) engaging in any action. The emotive 'I' is not linked to the students' action plan; rather the teacher uses it to define a place for himself in the mainstream class. I found a similar and related discursive move in language specialists' referring to tasks set by the subject specialists. Rather than owning the tasks through 'I', they referred to the tasks as if the tasks themselves had agency (see Creese, 1997 for examples). Another difference was the lack of an evaluative move by the language specialist in the usual initiation, response, feedback (evaluate) sequence identified by Sinclair and Courthard (1975).

In addition to these differences in the way language and subject specialists talk to the whole class, there were further differences in the way teachers drew on institutional structures to maintain their institutional statuses. Subject specialists referred to themselves as arbitrators of the exam system. They felt able to indicate to students what kind of grades they could achieve.

Extract Seven: *a) subject specialists; S = student, T = teacher*

S   I don't want to do that again.

T   You must do it. It is absolutely essential. This is where you'll get the A as opposed to the B, or the C as opposed to the D.

S   Sir, I'm not that clever.

T   Yes, you are that clever. And you should be working, you should be aiming for a top grade.

b) subject specialists; S = student, T = teacher,

T   You don't have to get everything done on it; obviously if you do, you are going to get a better mark. And you are very capable of getting a top grade in this aren't you? The only trouble is you muck about in the lessons too much, don't you? Yeah?

S   It's not my fault though, it is my surroundings, my atmosphere.

T   Perhaps it's not your fault but you have also to take responsibility for actually getting the work done, haven't you?

On the other hand, language specialists working in support mode were much more likely to draw on the subject teacher as their main link to institutional expertise.

Extract Eight: *language specialist*

Mr Roberts gets you all to make borders, doesn't he? Mr. Porter makes people make borders. Mr. Sullivan gets people to make borders. You put a border around that and it makes it look a hundred times better?

Here the lack of 'I' to ask the students to make borders perhaps indicates the lack of institutional support this language specialist feels for her own agendas.

A final discursive difference that was revealed between subject and language specialists across both partnership and support modes occurred in the giving of answers. I found that subject teachers were more likely than language specialists to give answers in one-to-one interactions. The reasons for this are complex and have as much to do with how teachers are judged successful, as they do with pedagogy and knowledge expertise.

Extract Nine: *subject specialist; S = student, T = teacher*

T   You can also say how you got around this line here. You know, instead of colouring it in with black felt, you actually put metal around it, didn't you? That's an important point.

S   Yeah.

T   You wanna say how you did that. That is important. And you wanna say about how you changed the size. Also put down about colour. You wanted it grey but we didn't have any grey so you had to have it black.

S   Right.

T   Get all those things down.

I found that language specialists, on the other hand, were much more likely to ask students a series of questions in order to guide them in achieving the task (see Creese, 1997 for examples). It is likely that the students themselves observed this differences in teacher action, as can be observed in the extract below.

Extract Ten: *language specialist; S = student, T = teacher*

S   Write it, Miss. Answer it.

T   No, you do the answer. I am giving you enough help, you have to do your own work, otherwise you're not learning.

S   I am learning.

T   You have got to learn how to do it. Copy them onto another piece of paper, then you draw this and finish the poster.

S   Miss, let's answer the questions now.

T   Well, you can do that yourself, I am not going to.

S   I...I can't.

T   Yes you can.

S   I can't.

T   (pause) I am not doing any more for you, I have done a lot for you already.

This refusal to give the answer to the student has a very good peda-gogical rationale. However, it also marks the language specialists' discursive practice as different from the subject teachers' in the study.

The discursive differences I have discussed in this section all help to position language specialists who work in support modes of col-laboration with subject teachers onto the periphery of the educa-tional mainstream. It is not that what the support teacher is doing is educationally unimportant for language-learning and curriculum-learning aims, but that in the mainstream content-based classrooms they are seen as peripheral aims. Support teachers and the subject teachers they work with are therefore contributing towards making language issues less important than other educational areas. Unless there is a radical shift in the way language work is planned in pri-mary and secondary schools (and there are many good arguments for such a shift) the only current way to make language work more mainstream is through partnerships with subject teachers.

Conclusion

Within the new EMAG framework, 'language issues' in schools can no longer be treated simply as 'support issues'. 'Language work' must interconnect the domains of the mental, social, cultural, institu-tional and political (Gee, 1999; Mercer, 1998). This interface will be the developing expertise of the language specialist. Part of my argu-ment in this chapter has been that a discourse of language support in schools helps create a restricted view of language as the servant to 'more important' learning aims. In my view, language and cultural diversity must be on the same platform as curriculum learning aims rather than somewhere behind them. If we accept this argument, we need to develop a newly articulated view of the expertise of lan-guage specialists which includes knowledge areas such as:

- language and power – particularly methodologies of critical discourse analysis

- language planning and policy – particularly studies which look at other multilingual and multicultural education settings along with their methodologies; an understanding of how 'macro' policies are played out in 'micro' practices

- language and culture – particularly classroom studies which view intellectual development as dialogic, interactive and culturally sensitive; a view of the classroom which sees pedagogy as constitutive of identity and cultural positionings as well as reflective of them

- language learning – particularly psycholinguistic classroom-based studies which look at bilingualism, multilingualism and second-language acquisition in content-based classrooms

This new knowledge will not be easily acquired. For one thing, EAL/TESOL is not recognised as a specialist subject area in initial teacher training. If it exists as an area at all, it is often as a subsidiary course to serve subject areas. There are no opportunities offered for practical teaching in subsidiary course subjects. Successful completion of an EAL subsidiary course does not give Qualified Teacher Status and is therefore not notified to the DfEE, which in turn means that it does not figure in the letter of qualification. Moreover, the Standards for the Award of Qualified Teacher Status (DfEE, 1998c) specifically mentions language twice only: first, that teachers need to be able to identify pupils who are not yet fluent in English and second, that teachers should [set] high expectations for all pupils notwithstanding individual differences, including gender, and cultural and linguistic backgrounds. Within mainstream educational policy, including the national curriculum, initial teacher education, the literacy strategy and the numeracy strategy, language work is ignored, forgotten or at best mentioned as an afterthought. Language tends to be subsumed under race and ethnicity, with differences in linguistic background ironed out in a discourse of equality. For the situation to be improved, language must feature more prominently in initial and continuing teacher training.

Another important issue is the need for long-term funding for EMAG. Short-term planning has led to short-term contracts with little opportunity, encouragement or initiative to develop a career in EAL, unlike, for example, special educational needs, which is underpinned by legislative support and which is embodied in the role of the SENCO.

Expertise in language, with its impact on the cultural, social, pedagogic and political dimensions of school life, is crucial in the richly diverse school communities of the multilingual and multicultural cities of today. Language expertise, like any knowledge expertise, cannot be viewed as static content residing somewhere comfortably in our minds, but must be seen as a process. As educationists we need to be constantly questioning and challenging knowledge hierarchies. If we view the classroom as a space for the 'construction of collective knowledge' in which knowledge is seen as resource, we can begin to see the importance of language and diversity in bringing different ways of viewing the world to the learning and teaching process (Scardamalia and Bereiter, 1999, p. 2). Learning and teaching are social activities, and as Kress (1995, 1996) has argued, teachers need to conceive of their students as having social needs which are inseparable from their linguistic identities.

In mainstream classrooms we need a view of language which helps us to manage and enjoy difference and diversity, not one that sees language as a problem which gets in the way of the one-way kind of learning. Support relationships contribute to individualist discourses, which isolate both teachers and students in peripheral positions in which their important educational concerns are sidelined. Partnerships, on the other hand, contribute to collaborative discourses and the creation of new hybrid discourses: both teachers and students learn through participation in these discourses. They are essential for effective EMAG work.

7

Bilingual learners and the Literacy Hour

Maggie Gravelle

The NLS has terrific potential, but it can also be a licence to be dull. (Year 6 teacher)

Introduction

The National Literacy Strategy (NLS) is relatively recent and research into its impact is therefore limited. The strategy framework (DfEE, 1998d) includes guidance on 'children with English as an additional language'. This guidance was published and distributed after the original framework document, partly as a response to teachers' concerns. It emphasises the inclusive nature of the strategy and attempts to offer support to teachers and specialist staff in order to make the Literacy Hour accessible for bilingual learners. The guidance suggests that teachers 'take full account of their [EAL pupils'] specific needs' (*ibid.* p. 106). However it offers no advice on the distinctive nature of bilingualism or of how these needs might be determined.

Instead it makes suggestions about the ways in which the organisation and activities within the Literacy Hour are suitable for bilingual learners, for example through revisiting texts, demonstrating the reading and writing processes and providing opportunities for talk. There are a number of examples about how particular activities can be used for bilingual learners. The guidance also has a brief section on ways of involving any additional adults who might be available to support bilingual pupils, but refrains from offering detailed advice about how they might offer that support.

The guidance acknowledges that bilingual pupils speak and may be literate in languages other than English. It also recognises that the term EAL covers a wide range of levels of English language fluency from beginners to those with 'native-like' fluency. It fails to give any recognition beyond this to the place of children's home languages in their identity and educational development, seeing them merely as tools in the acquisition of English.

Before publication of the framework, a consultation exercise invited comments on the first draft, but the final version of the document contained very few amendments. In response to the inadequacies identified being left unamended, a number of publications have offered suggestions for enabling bilingual learners to gain full benefit from the initiative. For example, *Provision in Literacy Hours for Pupils Learning English as an Additional Language* (NALDIC, 1998b) points out that bilingual learners have knowledge, understanding and skills in language which teachers should take into account. They also have needs in relation to English literacy which are not fully addressed by the framework and teachers will want ways of assessing these needs in order to plan appropriately.

Following on from this, NALDIC published a working paper about the distinctive nature of the language development of bilingual learners (NALDIC, 1999). Drawing extensively on the work of Cummins and other leading theorists, it points out that although there are similarities between first- and second-language acquisition, certain crucial differences require specific teaching strategies to support bilingual learners in gaining full access to the curriculum. It gives an outline of some pedagogical considerations such as the need to support the vocabulary, language structures, functions and grammar through modifying and supplementing existing materials.

A central feature of the literacy strategy, and one that is emphasised in the training, is interactive teaching. The National Literacy Project, which preceded the NLS, was based on research from countries such as Taiwan, Australia and the USA. It is generally agreed that genuinely interactive teaching, which allows children to contribute ideas and experiences in a secure environment, is supportive of bilingual learners; it provides them, and their peers, with opportunities to practice and extend their developing language skills and encourages collaboration and exploration. However, as Mroz, Hardman and Smith discuss, the concept of interactive teaching within the Literacy Hour is not necessarily of this nature (Mroz *et al,* forthcoming). It is, instead, characterised by teacher exposition, followed by teachers questioning pupils and giving some level of feedback. The model is one of teacher-direction rather than learner-control.

In principle, the NLS provides a clear structure on which to base the explicit language teaching that can support bilingual learners, although, as Sealey (1999) points out, there are some confusions and contradictions in its theoretical foundations. This view is supported by Beard, who, in summarising the research base and the evidence for the achievements of the NLS, draws on school effectiveness research (Beard, 1999). He also discusses the issues of teaching quality, referring extensively to OFSTED and HMI reports on literacy as well as to test results. He notes that one of the difficulties with using inspection evidence is that the criteria and framework within which assessments are made need to be questioned. This is confirmed by the evaluations carried out by OFSTED in 1998 and 1999, which comment on the extent to which the NLS is being implemented rather than on the value and validity of the structure itself. As both Cox (1998) and Hilton (1998) imply, much of the research quoted in support of the strategy is of a similar nature, in that it fails to question the underlying concept of what it means to be literate. This is of particular concern when considering the literacy development of bilingual learners, who may have very varied experiences, knowledge and skills.

The issue of children's needs and the account that should be taken of their histories is well illustrated in an article by Brennan and Taylor (1998). Through a number of case studies, they indicate the specific approaches that seemed successful in the development of literacy for bilingual learners. A ten-year-old girl of Portuguese descent had been labelled as having special educational needs after only a term and a half of British schooling. It was found that by building on her existing literacy in Portuguese she was able to demonstrate and improve her English language skills. An eight-year-old Somali refugee enjoyed reading and used contextual cues to provide meaning but lacked skills in phonics. However the case study suggests that his understanding of phonics needed to be firmly located in a whole-language approach. Talking and listening contributed to his developing literacy. There is ample evidence that bilingual learners are frequently skilled at 'barking at print' and yet this can disguise the fact that their understanding is in some cases severely limited.

The interim evaluation of the NLS mentions EAL pupils and suggests that practice varies and that 'many schools... are still debating how best to apply the structure of the literacy hour and make the most effective use of the available support'(OFSTED, 1998, p. 10). And yet as recently as 1996, the School Curriculum and Assessment Authority issued a booklet which gave very helpful advice to schools on effective teaching and planning, including the use of additional support in the classroom (SCAA, 1996). Many of these recommendations could be incorporated into the planning and teaching of the Literacy Hour and yet no reference is made to this publication in any of the documentation, nor are its suggestions developed in the framework.

In 1998 a report into teaching and learning strategies in successful multi-ethnic schools was published by the DfEE (Blair and Bourne, 1998). This mirrored in some ways the Medwell, Wray, Poulson and Fox report of the same year, *Effective Teachers of Literacy*, commissioned by the Teacher Training Agency (TTA) (Medwell *et al.*, 1998). Both reports identified successful teachers and schools and then investigated the aspects that were common among them. Blair and Bourne focused specifically on the achievements of ethnic minority students. Their findings suggest that there are several factors which make schools successful, whether or not they have a multi-ethnic intake, but that there are some features that are particular to schools with relatively large numbers of ethnic minority and bilingual pupils. Among these are the opportunities for learners to build on and develop their first language skills and their cultural identities. They claim that

> the most successful multi-ethnic schools develop practices which reveal respect, show the ability to listen and learn from students and their parents, to perceive the students' own cultures and the school ethos as students see them and are willing to reappraise and adapt school practices in the light of these. (Blair and Bourne, 1998, p. 170)

In April 1999, the Ethnic Minority Achievement Grant was introduced. The devolvement of funding, and to a large measure the responsibility, for the achievement of bilingual learners to heads and classroom teachers came at a time when primary teachers had already spent many hours planning for and implementing the Literacy Hour and the National Numeracy Strategy.

In the light of this new grant, this chapter reports on some initial observations of the implementation of the Literacy Hour and the provision for bilingual learners in several primary schools in one multi-ethnic inner-city LEA.[23] It is based on discussions with teachers and pupils and on observations during lessons. The heads and teachers volunteered to be part of the investigation because of their concern about provision for the bilingual children in their schools and classes. In addition, children and teachers give their views on the Literacy Hour and the provision for bilingual learners within it.

Teachers generally had a broad and positive view of the bilingual pupils in their classroom. Their definitions of 'bilingual' showed their understanding that it is a wide-ranging term applying to children with varied levels of literacy and fluency in a number of languages, including English. Several teachers explicitly mentioned that it included children whose English was totally fluent or who predominantly used English in the home but came from a different linguistic background and had access to other languages. They also recognised that the new funding gave them responsibility for children of African-Caribbean heritage, many of whom are born and educated in the UK but who need support for reasons of 'cultural assertion'. Only one of the teachers referred to her own bilingualism. 'I speak Gujerati, but I can't read or write it.'

Despite generally overestimating the number of bilingual learners in the school, they all talked positively about the impact that the presence of these pupils had on their practice and on the children in the class. Two, from the same school, discussed the practice of using a range of languages to greet children at registration.

> We say 'hello' in a lot of different languages in the morning, but I've never pressurised the children. I've asked the parents of the children who don't speak English what 'hello' is so that we can say it in Farsi or Albanian, but what happens first is that children are very reluctant to open up and I don't pressurise them. (teacher, Reception)

> It's not a big deal in the classroom. They know it's another language and they can use it. We have a different language each week. (teacher, Year 1)

Another, also from this school, described the high profile he tried to give to languages other than English. 'Children feel quite positive about the language they speak. Lots of them chose to write their names in their home language on the books they've just published' (teacher, Year 3). The presence of other languages is evident in this particular school in the notices, labels and children's work around the school. In some other schools, the impact is less obvious and staff are less informed about the linguistic and cultural background of their pupils. In some cases the lack of appropriate bilingual staff was blamed. 'Our bilingual classroom assistants speak Somali, Punjabi and Urdu... but there are about 37 different languages altogether' (teacher, Year 2).

Teachers were asked about the appropriateness of the strategies they used in the Literacy Hour and the particular provision they made for bilingual learners. Most of the Key Stage 1 teachers were enthusiastic about the structure that the NLS framework provided and felt that it enabled bilingual learners to participate and develop. The shared reading gave pupils good models and provided opportunities for explicit teaching and for promoting understanding. 'It's like being an actor, you have to use gestures and all sorts to keep them with you' (teacher, Year 1). A Year 6 bilingual pupil in the early stages of developing English echoed this when she said, 'I understand when I can see the pictures and the teacher uses different voices.'

Several teachers discussed the use of repetition and rhyme to support literacy development: 'The explicitness and repetitiveness of the Literacy Hour is very helpful' (teacher, Year 2). They also mentioned the constant use of visual clues and of other aids such as puppets. Children of this age who are still developing their language skills are 'quite open about it if they don't understand' (teacher, reception). The discussion and inclusive nature of the shared sessions made all the children comfortable but still some teachers still felt that the pace of sessions could leave bilingual learners behind. 'I think often there's no time to explain things fully' (teacher, Year 1). This teacher was concerned about a pupil at an early stage of developing English, whose lack of understanding and involvement was beginning to be made evident by her distracting behaviour.

At Key Stage 2, some teachers identified greater levels of difficulty. More children, they believed, had problems in understanding, and the pace of lessons as well as the abstract nature and complexity of some of the texts made it hard for teachers to provide the necessary support. 'I know that you should use props, but the reality is that I don't...that's just the thing that gets squeezed out' (teacher, Year 3). 'The level of text must be extremely confusing and...it isn't pre-sented in the same way as in the early years. It's much more what does this tell you about the character' (teacher, Year 6).

They were aware that not all children fully understood the texts and were worried about the lack of time for reinforcing concepts and understanding. 'Most of my children are very capable at decoding. The problem lies in comprehension' (teacher, Year 6). 'Year 6 teach-ing is more to do with comprehension and we do a lot of analysing and discussing meaning at all stages. My only concern is the pace' (teacher, Year 6).

There were differing views about the benefits of grammatical aspects of the NLS. One teacher said 'I think teaching grammar is difficult for bilingual learners because you want them to have a go without correcting every single thing...' (teacher, Year 6). Another: 'We talk about grammatical structures and understand grammatical terms. They [bilingual children] respond well to the explanations, better often than the English kids' (teacher, Year 6).

Many of the Key Stage 2 teachers talked about the importance of differentiation. In some schools, classes are ability-grouped for the whole of the Literacy Hour, particularly in Year 6. Teachers generally found this helpful and extra support was sometimes available for the group with most of the bilingual learners. While being aware of the possible dangers of setting, some teachers reported a rise in confidence among the bilingual pupils. 'They know they are a slower group but their self-esteem has grown immensely' (teacher, Year 6). This was attributed to the additional attention and to the progress the pupils made.

Additional support was often given by bilingual classroom assistants. There is a strong tradition in the authority studied of giving mother-tongue support. But the obverse is that teachers rely on this as the only appropriate help. Guided reading or writing and independent work, when additional support was most frequently used, were seen as presenting great difficulties for bilingual learners because of more limited access to meaning. None of the teachers offered suggestions for supporting meaning beyond the use of bilingual assistants or visual aids, although several emphasised the importance of talk and welcomed opportunities to use drama and role-play to develop meaning and response to text. The bilingual assistants generally saw their role as mediating between the teacher and the text. 'My role is to help them to learn what the teacher is teaching, not to focus on teaching them English' (bilingual classroom assistant). They used the mother tongue only to support understanding. 'The transitional use of the first language is very important' (teacher, Year 2).

Other teachers felt that placing bilingual learners in low-ability groups, often with children who had learning difficulties, gave a negative signal to other children and restricted their language experiences. 'It is usually the SEN group you put them with if you do it on ability' (teacher, Year 6). Mixed-ability grouping was seen as very beneficial, but rarely implemented. 'We sometimes break from ability groups and have gender splits or random partners. The bilingual children are not grouped all together' (teacher, Year 3). Mixed-ability grouping was seen to increase opportunities for talk, although no reference was made to planning for talk or to collaborative learning.

Talking about books was one of the features of the Literacy Hour that the children said they enjoyed. Bilingual learners in Year 2 were keen to share their reading with a friend and to join in the shared reading. When they had the opportunity to choose a book to read outside the Literacy Hour, several children talked freely and related the text to their own experiences. They were confident about their own reading ability, even when their understanding seemed to be limited, and talked about reading at home as well as at school.

Older children were more reflective and could not only discuss their choice of book but also anticipate endings and discuss characters and story forms. 'Stories like that always have happy endings' (pupil, Year 6). They found the explanations given by the teacher and the opportunities for modelling and shared writing very helpful. They also remarked on the fact that shared reading gave them access to more difficult books than they might tackle alone. One boy acknowledged his limitations, 'I can read hard books, but sometimes I don't know what they mean' (pupil, Year 6). In another school, a boy remarked that he did not always understand the words the teacher used and seldom answered questions because he felt he was being tested. Children also commented on the ability grouping, some feeling that they were misplaced and had little opportunity to change. They discussed working with partners or on their own but opinion differed as to which was preferable.

There is considerable evidence that continuing to use first language is supportive both of understanding and of English language development. The class teachers, while recognising the significance of home languages to the children as individuals, felt able to do little more than acknowledge this. 'The bilingual assistant would stay for story time and tell the story in Turkish. The children loved it' (teacher, Year 1). Bilingual teachers and assistants felt that opportunities to maintain or even develop mother tongue were limited. 'I read them books in Somali so they can hear their own language' (bilingual class room assistant). 'There are two that share the same language but choose not to use it' (teacher, Year 3).

Similarly, the children felt there was little opportunity or encouragement for using their first languages in the school. 'I'm quite shy to speak my language' (pupil, Year 6). 'I speak the languages of my friends, but only with them' (pupil, Year 6). Only one girl, whose mother tongue was French, had the confidence to make a contribution when asked to translate and was proud to do so.

Observations during Literacy Hour

We have come to expect primary classrooms to be bright and lively, with displays of children's work and various aspects of literacy. These classrooms were no exception. In several schools there were dual-language books and multilingual signs and in one classroom it was evident that Chinese New Year had just been celebrated. In some of the sessions extra support was available, in some cases specifically for bilingual learners and in other cases an extra adult to work with a group of pupils. In one school, the bilingual children were withdrawn for the independent part of the hour to work with a trained teacher.

All the Literacy Hours observed followed the pattern prescribed by the framework. In all cases they began with a shared reading session in which bilingual children were expected to join. In two of the sessions, the support teacher participated and worked with two of the most needy bilingual children, intervening to explain or to confirm their own contributions. In one case, the two children in question were actively engaged with the task, answering questions, reading alongside the teacher and offering reasons for their ideas. The only other bilingual child in this class did not participate actively but appeared to be listening carefully and following the reading. She seemed to lack confidence in her understanding and often glanced round at the other children to check their responses.

In the other supported class, the support teacher used her first language to explain what was required and then helped two girls to write initial sounds on their white boards. Some of the other bilingual children in this class were involved in the shared reading and answered questions, although towards the end they became distracted and started looking around the room and fidgeting. It was noticeable that several of them relied on watching other children before committing themselves to a response.

In a Year 6 class, the shared word-level work explored suffixes in which the more fluent bilingual pupils were actively engaged. However, several other children seemed not to follow the explanations or to participate in the activities. During the group work, there was an additional teacher who took responsibility for some of the bilingual learners. But although he answered direct questions and gave reassurance to the children who had made some attempt at engaging with the work, he appeared not to have any specific plans or supportive strategies for the bilingual learners. On one occasion two of the girls were playing a 'joining the dots' game for six or seven minutes before he intervened.

In classes where some support was available for bilingual pupils at an early stage of English language acquisition and where the adult was trained and had a specific role with regard to these children, there was at least some opportunity for them to engage with the tasks and understand the text. Where this was not the case, or when pupils were no longer receiving support, the children had to operate as best they could.

This 'sink or swim' situation prevailed to a large extent in other classes observed. In a Year 3 class, the session began with some role-play which gave all the children a chance to become involved and to talk to each other in and out of role. The teacher of this class had said that his 'worst nightmare would be going into a classroom and the children are sitting quietly and not talking'. Accordingly, his lessons were highly interactive. He was sufficiently sensitive to ask appropriate questions and give children confidence in their responses. He also modelled the subsequent independent task through a shared writing activity. During the group work, he concentrated on one group of children and monitored their understanding closely. So over the course of a week, all the pupils would have benefited from his attention. However the bilingual support teacher for this class worked with an individual pupil for only half an hour a week. Except for the guided group, many of the children took time to settle to their independent activities and their progress seemed to rely almost entirely on self-motivation.

The same was largely true of the reception class. During the animated shared reading of *The Little Red Hen*, most children were listening, following the text and responding. All the children were given encouragement and guidance and most of them stayed on-task for the full half-hour. But independent work proved to be far less supportive of the bilingual children, whose concentration lapsed after a very short time. The tasks that had been devised showed no evidence of being planned with the needs of bilingual learners in mind.

The most successful independent work took place in a Year 1 class where the teacher had planned the activities carefully, had differentiated widely and had taken considerable time and effort to ensure that all the children understood the task. The activities followed closely on the shared reading, which was based on a non-fiction text. The teacher had been at pains to reinforce understanding of the text, supporting it well with visuals and with the children's existing and shared experiences. During this session, all the bilingual pupils were interested and engaged. They asked and answered questions and completed activities which were appropriate for their linguistic and cognitive level.

Conclusions

All the teachers in this study had positive attitudes towards bilingual learners and made conscious efforts to include them in all activities, including the Literacy Hour. Many of them were well informed and interested and some had taken part in extra training in the past. One was herself bilingual. Their positive attitude was conveyed to all the children and was to a certain extent reflected in the resources, including first languages, that were drawn on.

In addition these were experienced and skilled teachers who, although they may have had varying views of the NLS, were all committed to giving the children a positive and fulfilling learning experience. Much of the observed success of the Literacy Hours relied on this skill and commitment; and in general it could be said that the bilingual pupils were at least as engaged and interested as the majority of their peers.

On the other hand, there was little evidence of specific planning to meet the needs of the bilingual pupils. Such support as was available in the form of specialist teachers was, at best, used to give some additional explanation and reinforcement to a small number of 'early-stage learners'. In several cases, the extra adult spent much time either following the teacher's lead or being relatively passive, particularly in the shared part of the hour. With the exception of one former Section-11 teacher, there was no evidence of any joint planning, sharing or collaboration by the support teacher and the class teacher. This was due both to pressure of time and to time-tabling constraints, resulting in the extra adult being expected to work for short periods of time with as many individual pupils as possible. There was no evidence of any parental support and in fact one teacher mentioned that the level of involvement by parents had diminished since the introduction of the NLS.

The EAL guidance in the NLS framework suggests reasons why the structure and approach is appropriate for bilingual learners. In the absence of an alternative, most teachers seem to accept this, particularly when their pupils had already developed a certain level of fluency in English. Any difficulties children might have with understanding complex texts or using sophisticated language structures appeared to be explained by their ability rather than their English proficiency. This resulted in the seeming 'invisibility' of all but the least fluent pupils. Although several teachers expressed concern at the problems some texts might present, particularly at Key Stage 2, there was no evidence that they either knew how to make it comprehensible or had the time or resources to do so. In support of this view, many of the strategies such as collaborative talk, the use of role-play, complementing and supplementing text, charts, diagrams and other key visuals, encouraging first language and making concepts concrete, were not in evidence. What differentiation there was served largely to group many bilingual pupils together, sometimes with children of low ability.

None of this was due to lack of interest or concern on the part of the teachers, although some of it may have been due to lack of training. The Literacy Hour gives even these teachers little opportunity to match the pace and content of their teaching to the needs of the pupils. There was insufficient time for children to talk, to share experiences and understanding, to repeat and rehearse, to return and consolidate, to take control of their own learning or to extend their creativity. The time for teachers to plan together, to enjoy and pursue enthusiasms, to collect or produce suitable resources or to deviate from the relentless pursuit of objectives and targets was severely limited. Whether specific extra funding from EMAG will improve matters remains an open question. As Patricia Rowan has remarked: 'You can hit your target and still miss the whole point of the operation' (Rowan, 2000).

8

'At the edge of Being': managing **EMAG** in classrooms and schools

Roger West

Never being, but always at the edge of Being
(Stephen Spender, *Preludes 10*)

I spotted Ahmed straight away in his nursery class in south-east London. He was the one right over on the far side of the room by the window. In his hands he held a few pieces of a jigsaw puzzle which he was studying with bewilderment. It seemed that it wasn't just that he didn't know how to fit the pieces together, but that he wasn't sure what these objects were actually for. I could see his lips moving and asked his teacher what language he spoke. 'Gobbledygook', she said. She told me that he spent a lot of time apart from the rest of the children 'muttering to himself'. I went over to him and put my head very close to hear what he was saying. What he was saying, over and over again very softly to himself was 'Oh dear, oh dear, oh dear, oh dear'.

If you want to find the bilingual learners in their schools, that's often where they will be – out on the edges of their classrooms, on the peripheries of the playground, pinned against the wire netting as if by some centrifugal force, wondering how just to be within the educational context let alone how to learn anything. This is hardly surprising for these are the pupils who have always been on the edges of educational policy and practice – the appendices to policy documents, the footnotes to reports, the annotations in the margins of legislation. They are in danger of always being the ESL – the educationally subliminal.

Is this deliberate? Is the agenda to withhold provision from these children and deny them access to learning? Education is a way for the dominant group in society to retain social control, and its policies are a deliberate expression of that. This dominant group may be the capitalist elite (Hatcher and Troyna, 1994), a collection of a number of different groups or classes (Dale and Ozga 1991) or perhaps a collection of individual 'actors' (Ball, 1990). The first analysis would see the construction of education policy as the product of a quite definite agenda; the second would see it as the synthesis of different interests and tensions; the third would see it as a completely haphazard and accidental process. Experience has inclined me towards the last, although set within the context of the ethos of capitalism at a macro-level and of jealousy, spite and personal ambition at a micro-level.

In a recent interview, Kenneth Baker, the Education Secretary in Margaret Thatcher's government, admitted that the policies that resulted in the 1988 Education Reform Act, far from being based on a clear ideology of 'standards, freedom and choice' (Ribbins and Sherratt, 1997), were more the product of guesswork, whim and political infighting. Years of working for local authorities has made it depressingly obvious to me just how much policy is similarly reactive, rather than proactive, and often made up on the spur of the moment or at the last minute.

This is particularly so in the case of policies to do with children with English as an additional language (EAL), provision for whom has long been based on external funding which has been erratic, uncertain, short term and insufficient. Since 1992, most provision has come via Section-11-funded three-year projects, which have had to be match-funded by LEAs and therefore have frequently been been at the mercy of their frequent financial crises. The new EMAG funding arrangements have now reduced this to an annual funding cycle while the DfEE has been attempting – and failing – to come up with a nationally applicable formula to distribute this grant.

In the absence of any knowledge or understanding of how to meet the needs of children with EAL needs, the policy makers and providers at both national and local level still all too often take practice suitable for children with special educational needs and apply it to children with EAL needs. EAL practitioners have fought long and hard over the years to make the point that there is a huge difference between the needs of children who are unable to access the curriculum because of lack of fluency in the language in which it is presented and those unable to access it because of specific learning difficulties, and that a totally different approach is needed to supporting the learning of these two groups. And while there may be a recognition of this fundamental difference, organisational practice and inertia frequently keep them linked in people's minds. The guidance sent to schools on making special arrangements for pupils in national tests and for making temporary exceptions to the national curriculum, for example, takes children with learning difficulties as its reference point and then suggests that the same arrangements or procedures could be happily applied to children with EAL needs.

To add to the confusion, we are now being presented with government policies and guidance on 'inclusion'. This is a term which been used for some years now in the context of bringing children with SEN into mainstream schools and classes, but has recently come to encompass children from ethnic minority backgrounds, including those with EAL needs (QCA, 2000). This rhetoric not only assumes that including children with EAL needs into the mainstream requires a broadly similar approach to including those with SEN, but it also ignores the whole debate about assimilation and presents the notion of 'inclusion' as unproblematic. There are areas of debate here which are being ignored and which need to be considered and tackled before we drag our bilingual learners off the edges and into this bright, new, inclusive future. Including children does not mean not withdrawing them – we have to consider what it is we are including them into. The notion of one big, all-encompassing, all-inclusive mainstream is a popular one with the present Labour administration, but there is still the question of whether we want the mainstream to be a homogeneous or a pluralist one. And finally, if we accept that there will always be children on the edges, should we not be considering how to make them feel all right about being there?

The new EMAG arrangements can be seen as an attempt to bring EAL practice more into the mainstream. One criticism of the usual model of Section 11 provision – centrally organised and managed LEA teams of support staff allocated to schools on the basis of a need determined by the team managers – was that the work of its practitioners was separated from the life of the school and not necessarily responsive to its needs (OFSTED, 1999): operating, in other words, from out on the edges. The devolving of funds directly to schools would, in theory, allow headteachers to make their own decisions about the best use of the money to raise the attainment of their particular ethnic minority children and integrate the staff they employed more fully into the fabric of the school. The guidelines accompanying the new arrangements are apparently straightforward enough: the LEA comes up with a formula for the internal distribution of the grant that is fair, transparent and agreed by all. Schools then produce an action plan to show how they will use their share to raise ethnic minority achievement and the LEA monitors that the grant is being spent properly and to best effect (DfEE, 1998e).

There is, however, a fundamental problem with these guidelines and it is one that is rooted in the education policies of the last 20 years. This period has seen the shackling of the concept of the market to education and the application of its principles to education policy and legislation. However, even early on, a split started to emerge within the Thatcher government, between the neo-liberals, who stood for market radicalism, and the neo-conservatives, who stood for authority and tradition. The 1988 Education Act has been represented as the product of a compromise between these two elements. Although some of its measures increased school autonomy and parental choice, others were devoted to the setting up of a national curriculum, and many of the powers that were removed from LEAs ended up in the hands of the Education Secretary (Ribbins and Sherratt, 1997).

It can be argued that these powers were only transferred to central government temporarily as part of the process of ultimately devolving them (Johnson, 1991). But this transfer has created a tension between centralisation and devolution that has yet to be resolved. One possible way of dealing with it, if not resolving it, is to produce documents that give the appearance of being instructions that have to be followed to the letter, but which are in fact guidelines loose and vague enough to be interpreted in whatever way the reader chooses – provided of course he/she realises that this is so. The national curriculum was a case in point. What seemed at first to be content was only a suggested content to cover the attainment targets. Legislation thus creates a climate of enabling rather than coercion but appears to give schools and LEAs very little choice.

The EMAG guidelines fit into this pattern. They are woolly and full of statements of implication and expectation masquerading as instructions. They create gaps which allow schools and LEAs to further their short-term political and financial goals or the personal ambitions of key people. I could go on to discuss those LEAs which have abdicated all responsibility for their bilingual learners and which equate the notion of monitoring how schools are spending their allocated funds solely with financial auditing: it doesn't matter what the money is spent on as long as they have the receipts. I could also discuss schools where nobody knows how much EMTAG money they have received or what it is being used for, and where experienced EAL teachers are having their contracts terminated to allow headteachers to buy job lots of classroom assistants.

However, I want this to be a positive piece, so in this chapter I look instead at the gaps in the DfEE EMAG guidelines and how they can be exploited to the advantage of bilingual learners. We can use them to the advantage of our bilingual learners, The integration of EAL support staff into schools has opened up all sorts of opportunities for working with colleagues and therefore all sorts of possibilities for exciting and innovative work with bilingual learners.

Good headteachers will be looking at how to use their grant to build up a team which has the right background, interests and expertise to match the needs of the school and its ethnic minority population. They may need to keep this initially as a shadow structure and look in the short term at making the best possible use of existing staffing. A likely scenario is that such schools will have EMAG teams consisting of an experienced EAL support teacher plus a number of classroom assistants, with other teachers topping up their existing mainstream or support commitments with some EMAG work. The experienced EAL support teacher will then find herself in a leadership role, having to supervise, co-ordinate and perhaps even line manage the work of a disparate collection of individuals with different perspectives and levels of understanding of the EAL needs of children and with conflicting and contrasting commitments elsewhere in the school.

EMAG co-ordinators are increasingly having to take on line management responsibilities – sometimes without the status, recognition and salary scale of a line manager. They might not have planned to take that route but perhaps had to because of structural changes; they might then have found themselves having to cope with a role which had arisen in a haphazard way and whose function, purpose, duties and responsibilities had not been clearly defined. In a recent study of women EAL co-ordinators with line management responsibilities, working in central teams and in schools, I found that these co-ordinators were redefining management and leadership to make it more appropriate to the particular area they found themselves working in. This area was one that has been largely conducted on the edges of the mainstream and so they were constructing new models of management from ideas, experiences, knowledge and practices from outside their immediate professional role (West, 1998).

It was clear that what was happening was the emergence of new models of management that fitted in more comfortably with the role of support teacher, based on concepts of empowering, facilitating, enabling and motivating and drawing on the roles of skilled helper, supervisor and mentor. Management is about containing, whereas leadership is about moving people forward (Kerry and Murdoch, 1993). Good EAL teachers have always been concerned with moving mainstream practice forward and often have had to do this without the line management status to legitimate their efforts. As leaders of EMAG teams in schools they will now be able to draw upon and enhance their work with bilingual learners and to explore creative, imaginative and lateral ways to support these pupils' learning.

To conclude, I would like to look at five areas which I believe are the key ones for bringing bilingual children away from the edges and into the mainstream and which afford opportunities for creative approaches to raising their achievement.

1. Make children the experts

Bilingual learners will never be able to operate effectively in the mainstream if they feel disempowered. If knowledge is power, we need to ensure they have knowledge. And one way to do this is to re-conceptualise knowledge as something they already have and not just something they do not have and have yet to acquire. The multi-cultural approaches to teaching from the 1970s have quite rightly identified the lack of engagement many children have with a curri-culum that is culturally alien. This understanding led to initiatives to make the curriculum more relevant by introducing role models, examples and artefacts drawn from the cultures of the children in the classroom. This produced some exciting work but also some dreary materials. Mary Seacole may, for example, be a more appropriate role model for most of the class than Florence Nightingale, but if the text about her is inaccessible and the activities uninspiring, little is accomplished.

Bilingual learners have a wealth of skills, knowledge, interests and perspectives that can be shared with other pupils and which can cast them in the role of the expert. This has to be done within an ethos of respect and sensitivity, however, otherwise it could backfire. Not all bilingual learners will feel safe or comfortable about sharing aspects of their culture and background with others and it is important to recognise that they do not always have to be called upon as the expert in their own culture – they can be the experts in all sorts of other areas that are not culturally specific. To set them up as them-selves cultural artefacts will confine them to the edges. There is a similar point to be made about the use of bilingual support teachers, who all too often are only called upon to do support work with chil-dren who share their language, or to do translation work, thus deny-ing them the recognition of having many other skills and talents.

2. Provide opportunities for talk

Bilingual learners, it has often been said, go through a 'silent period' when they are processing the sounds, rhythms and structures of English before they gain the confidence to start to speak it: they therefore need as much exposure to spoken English as possible. This may indeed be going on, but bilingual learners do not always do this processing silently; they may be highly vocal as they try out sounds, words and inflections for themselves. A number of writers have pointed to the importance of language use in language development (Gibbons, 1991). Passively receiving English will not enhance learning it as much as interacting in it will, so the inclusive classroom needs to provide opportunities for bilingual learners to engage in such interactions. And if learning occurs through talk, the interactions need to be focused around learning activities. It is important here to recognise the distinction between group activities which do not allow opportunities for all children to participate and which can equally well be carried out by children working on their own, although grouped around the same table, and those which are genuinely interactive and collaborative. Examples of these include problem-solving and information-sharing activities whose success depends on the contributions of *all* participants.

A final word about grouping. Despite an increasing trend towards streaming and setting, children are still often arranged in mixed-ability groups, with the bilingual learners either scattered throughout the groups or in a separate group. Management studies research about what makes effective teams has identified the different roles needed in any team. It might be worthwhile to consider applying this approach to setting up groups for interactive tasks.

3. Find out what strategies children are using to support their own learning

Most bilingual learners want to make sense of what is happening in the classroom. They want to come away from the edges and to feel comfortable and secure in the classroom. They want their school experience to be a meaningful one. They will therefore use every strategy at their disposal to achieve this. The best way teachers can support their bilingual learners is to notice what strategies the children themselves are using and favouring and to build on them. This requires teachers to stand back and observe children. They must also talk to them about these strategies and listen to what they say. They must then facilitate these strategies and may also need to legitimate them for those children who think they might not be allowed.

4. Work with parents to support their children's learning

Many schools have good systems of communication with parents, often backed up by translation and interpreting services. However, this is still often a one-way communication; parents are only contacted when there is information to impart or a problem to sort out and sometimes they are brought in as cultural artefacts. It is important for teachers to find ways of working with parents so that both can support the children's learning in a coherent and seamless way. This means finding out what experiences, understanding and expectations parents have of schooling and what they perceive the purpose of education to be.

5. Have high expectations of children

Children, as we all know, will live either up or down to the expectations we have of them. Where the maintaining of high expectations often stands or falls is in the way children's progress is assessed. This is generally by reference to progress through stages of English fluency or by national curriculum attainment levels. The latter is the measure by which government targets are set and the former is still – despite attempts by the DfEE and OFSTED to discredit it – used as indicator of effective learning support in schools. The problem with both of these measures is that they do not show the rapid progress over a very short time that bilingual learners can make. They therefore do not allow teachers to see their real progress and attainment and this makes it difficult for teachers to sustain high expectations. I would like to suggest a number of indicators of progress that are applicable to such bilingual learners:

- increased confidence in speaking

- increased tendency to initiate interactions

- increased confidence is using physical space in the class-room and playground

- an increased tendency to take risks in interactions

- greater level of participation in whole-school activities

- greater independence in learning

- deeper retention of the content of lessons over time and a greater ability to discuss this content

- greater ability to identify their own cognitive processes and preferred strategies for learning

- greater enjoyment of the learning process

- evidence of discussions of learning activities with family members.

So whether EMAG will benefit children like Ahmed remains to be seen, but it very much depends on how we exploit the arrangements. As practitioners we are still, like some of the bilingual learners we support, on the edges of mainstream practice. We need to start striding boldly and fearlessly towards the mainstream. If it won't include us, we'll include it.

9
Repositioning EAL:
the way forward

Charlotte Franson

The new century marks a critical time for EAL practitioners in schools and for the field of EAL at large in the English context. In view of the changes and developments in funding as a result of the move to EMAG, how will EAL provision be positioned within the changing educational context? This chapter presents a discussion of some of the underlying assumptions and beliefs about EAL provision that have informed the past decade and suggests possible action for a future agenda.

Background
In the 1960s much of the provision offered to the many newly arrived immigrant children was predicated upon the English as a foreign language (EFL) teaching tradition and this generally entailed a classroom and/or a programme outside the mainstream classroom and curriculum (Edwards, 1983). Funding was provided through Section 11 of the 1966 Local Government Act. It was perceived that additional English language support would facilitate integration into mainstream schooling and, as at the time the predominant teaching model was informed by British EFL teaching, the additional teaching was directed at developing pupils' English language knowledge and skills to enable them to join the mainstream curriculum (Edwards and Redfern, 1992).

But by the early 1970s there was a move pedagogically and ideologically into mainstream provision. This was in response to the continuing needs of what were termed ESL (English as a second language) learners (DES, 1972) as they progressed through the curriculum. Ideologically, it was deemed important to integrate the second-language learner into the school, socially, culturally and academically. By the mid 1980s a more socio-cultural view of EAL learning predominated, as distinct from a psycholinguistic view. The influence of functional-communicative approaches in second-language education challenged the specialist role of the English-teaching expert (Levine, 1990, p. 22). Pedagogical support for the 'meaningful context' of the language-rich classroom for EAL learners was also found in second-language learning theories and communicative teaching approaches within the field of English language teaching (ELT). The value and importance of the home language and culture was highlighted in the Bullock Report (DES, 1975). And so EAL teachers found themselves working more and more within the mainstream classroom. Larger urban centres developed ESL teaching services that were very productive and energetic in promoting multicultural teaching. They emphasised social and cultural integration as well as antiracism through their support for ethnic and linguistic minority pupils in schools.

In 1988, the national curriculum was introduced. Despite the initiatives to indicate the distinctive language learning needs of bilingual pupils, the national curriculum orders reduced the more explicit references to the language and learning needs of EAL pupils to six points in the non-statutory guidance on English (DES and Welsh Office, 1990). Emphasis was placed upon 'access to the curriculum' and providing the same curriculum opportunities for all pupils. The results of the inquiry in Calderdale in the late 1980s by the Commission for Racial Equality (CRE, 1986), also endorsed the practice of 'mainstreaming'.

At the same time, the Home Office was conducting its scrutiny of the use of Section 11 funding (Home Office, 1989). It was apparent that changes to funding and the use of grant were impending. The final report of the Home Office scrutiny noted that 'At its best, ESL emphasised supporting language development as part of learning in other subjects as diverse as mathematics, physical education and nature studies' (Ibid, p. 42). As a result of this exercise, new bids were submitted for projects that took a distinctly mainstream approach to EAL provision. The early 1990s also saw the promotion of 'partnership teaching' and the collaboration of the EAL teacher with the mainstream classroom/subject teacher within the meaningful context of the mixed-ability classroom (Bourne and McPake, 1991 and also Angela Creese's Chapter 6 above). The new Section 11 grant criteria, with its emphasis on mainstreaming EAL provision, strengthened this positioning of EAL teachers as supporting colleagues in the mainstream classroom.

Mainstreaming

For many EAL teachers, mainstreaming was to be welcomed, for it would not only provide equality for ethnic and linguistic minority pupils but would also strengthen their position within the school. EAL teachers were given specific job descriptions which, for many, greatly helped in asserting their role in schools. They now had objectives and targets as well as evaluation by government through annual reports based on the learner's progression against certain criteria. However, the financial insecurity, caused because projects were dependent upon both central and matched local funding, engendered feelings of anxiety and insecurity. And as the remit of the Section 11 teacher widened over the years to include pupils of non-New-Commonwealth heritage without additional grant, and to take on other projects such as the training of mainstream teachers of bilingual pupils, the Section 11 projects came under increasing strain.

In their attempts to gain credibility for themselves and for the pupils they supported, EAL teachers not only worked alongside colleagues but contributed to various school activities such as playground duty and supply teaching, as well as acting as home-school liaison teachers, admissions teachers and so forth. Some schools took advantage of EAL teachers' willingness to become part of the mainstream and used them in a variety of roles. But many EAL teachers argued for a more prominent participatory role, stating that it gave them and their pupils credibility, and challenged the image of the

EAL teacher as in 'the cupboard under the stairs'. In many ways, the language-teaching role became secondary to the role of facilitator of cultural and social inclusion.

Developments in second language teaching methodology in the 1980s, which advocated meaningful communication (see, for example, Dulay *et al.*, 1982), were supported by the very nature of the English classroom, with its emphasis on peer interaction, group work, and activity- and inquiry-based learning. The mainstream classroom context was seen as a positive learning environment for the development of language knowledge and skills for the EAL learner. It was assumed that plenty of exposure, practice within a meaningful context and opportunities for purposeful uses of language would be sufficient. And the mainstream classroom was perceived as being a provider of all of these.[25]

EAL teachers have been very successful in promoting the notion of mainstreaming to the exclusion of other forms of provision. In the wider educational arguments about inclusion within the field of special educational needs, a similar debate continues. Some professionals feel that if pupils with special educational needs were to be included within mainstream provision, the feelings of difference and separateness associated with segregated provision would be reduced, and these pupils would benefit from interaction with other pupils. Also, other pupils within mainstream provision would learn to live more comfortably with diversity. For the EAL teachers and pupils, mainstreaming also includes learning about and living with linguistic and cultural diversity.

Yet in promoting mainstreaming, the profession has perhaps denied its sense of identity and deprived some EAL pupils of the specialist support that would have facilitated and accelerated their participation in the mainstream curriculum. Many EAL teachers argue that a single pedagogical approach does not suit the learning needs of all EAL pupils. Simply locating the EAL pupil in the mainstream classroom is not enough. Indeed, some recent ethnographic studies suggest that the complex interplay of variables in the classroom makes that assumption less secure (Toohey, 1998 and Willett, 1995).

For secondary-aged learners, individual, focused language tuition within a subject area can be very productive, and for newly arrived beginners, separate introductory language lessons can enable them to cope with the daily classroom demands. Providing separate lessons for EAL is not necessarily any different from having a separate history or science lesson. But this view has been considered almost as heresy by many in the profession, even though such lessons happen daily in the corner of the classroom, in the library session or in the corridor. Having situated the EAL pupil and teacher in the classroom and recognised the importance of the peer group and of contextualised language learning, it is also important also to recognise that the EAL learner has distinctive needs. In the zeal with which mainstreaming has been adopted (Edwards and Redfern, 1992), these needs have sometimes been lost. In terms of equality and inclusion, the profession should reconsider what conditions would positively *enable* EAL learners to participate equally in the curriculum.

Professional development

The EAL profession needs to examine and evaluate its work critically in order to develop a professional consensus on key issues pertinent to the teaching and learning of bilingual pupils. But this cannot be achieved if there is no commonality of professional training for EAL teachers. There also needs to be research into the development of professional training appropriate to the British context.

However, one could argue that mainstreaming has delayed the development of both training and research. The RSA Diploma course that many EAL teachers studied in the 1980s was no longer widely available by the early 1990s. The Home Office provided an institutional framework for Section 11 practice but not a forum for professional development and debate at a national level. However, most Section 11 projects developed some form of in-service training for their EAL and classroom teachers and some projects made links with local higher education institutions. In the mid 1990s the government provided funding for locally organised in-service training but targeted mainstream classroom teachers rather than the EAL teachers. Many EAL teachers took part in the training as both students and providers. Nevertheless, opportunities for both initial and continuing professional development have been limited and what has been offered has often been highly contextualised: urban centres with a high density of EAL learners have developed different approaches from those used in suburban and rural areas, where the pupils are fewer and more scattered amongst schools.

More recently, there have been initiatives to develop specialist training, with a few higher education institutions offering modules and programmes of study relevant to the teaching and learning of EAL pupils. The DfEE has commissioned research into standards or descriptors for EAL specialist teachers, and NALDIC, a professional association which has been actively promoting issues related to EAL teaching and learning, along with other such organisations, has provided a professional forum for EAL teachers through conferences, seminars and publications.

Yet there has been little challenge to existing practice or to the assumptions and beliefs that underpin current practice. Ideologically and politically, discussion of EAL provision has often been polarised: mainstreaming versus withdrawal; language specialist versus a wider school remit for social and cultural inclusion; and more recently, targeted funding versus more generalised funding. One might argue that the lack of training and professional development within the profession has contributed to these tensions. The challenge is to find a way in which these competing tensions can be managed better to support the teaching and learning of EAL pupils.

The role of the EAL teacher

There has been limited debate regarding the distinctiveness of the EAL teacher's role and that of the EAL learner. Bourne offered four definitions of an English language support teacher which included the specialist role, but the preferred model over the past decade seems to have been a combination of the roles of 'good teacher' and 'catalyst for change' within the school (Bourne, 1989). In practice most language support teachers have found that their role is largely determined by the school and classroom context in which they are working. A central concern has been the maintenance of good working relationships with their mainstream colleagues.

The view was held that any teacher could be an EAL teacher and those working in the field at the time did indeed come from a range of backgrounds. Many EAL teachers received their training on the job or through in-service training provided by their LEA language support service. The problem with this was that the process of training could become incestuous, limited by its lack of external input and interaction. Opportunities for research into EAL provision nationally, which could have led the profession forward more proactively, have also been limited.

One reaction on the part of EAL teachers to this lack of research, development and documentation of EAL practice at the national level was the adoption of practice from Australia, which in the 1980s and 1990s had developed a strong and informed voice in ESL provision. Books such as *Learning to Learn in a Second Language* by Pauline Gibbons continue to be popular (Gibbons, 1991) and in the past two or three years an in-service programme for mainstream teachers of EAL learners, also from Australia, has been taken up by a number of LEAs.

There were other difficulties for EAL teachers in establishing their role within the school. Perceptions developed over many years were hard to overcome and many EAL teachers continued to feel marginalised and undervalued. They continued to do other things besides teach EAL learners, including being used as supply cover, about which many complained but, because of their peripheral position in many schools, often without success. And this continued partly because the work of EAL teachers was not clearly defined and articulated. Despite being in the classroom and despite their best efforts to be considered as equal to their class/subject colleagues, many EAL teachers continued to lack status within schools (Franson, 1995).

So the wide remit has become a two-edged sword. On the one hand, there is the EAL teacher as a 'collaborative partner' working alongside mainstream colleagues, a teacher who is able to address a range of issues at whole-school level, and is also able to provide some discrete language teaching. Edwards and Redfern (1992) refer to the 'zealous' adherence to mainstreaming and partnership teaching. On the other hand, in taking this position, EAL teachers have relinquished much of their role as the language teaching specialist.

More recent initiatives indicate a new trend in government thinking and policy development. These initiatives include the devolution of funding and responsibility for EAL provision to schools through the Standards Fund, the widening of the scope of grant to include the raising of achievement in general of ethnic minority pupils and the inclusion, for a couple of years, of Traveller provision. Indeed, a significant indicator of the changes was the renaming of the funding for EAL provision as Ethnic Minority and Traveller Achievement Grant (EMTAG). EAL is being subsumed within the broad notion of 'raising achievement'. In this context, EAL teachers may find their role even more diffuse and less focused on the language and learning needs of EAL pupils. One example of this diffusion of role has been the merging of EAL and literacy support in some LEA services.

Informally, there is a great deal of agreement on what constitutes the role of the EAL teacher. Work on establishing descriptors for the EAL demonstrated a consensus amongst those who participated in the discussions and survey questionnaire.[26] Yet EAL teachers continue to have only limited opportunities for professional and career development. Blair and Bourne (1998) make this point explicitly in their report on teaching and learning in successful multi-ethnic schools.

Equally, EAL teachers need to keep informed of the research about teaching and learning English as a second or additional language.

Access and inclusion

At the end of the 1980s, LEAs had been through a period in which multicultural and antiracist teaching policies and strategies had been implemented. Government funding had been provided for 'multicultural education' initiatives and 'equality of access' had become a populist phrase. EAL teachers argued that mainstreaming was providing equality of access and saw their presence in the school as supporting their pupils' access to the curriculum. Elsewhere, merely mainstreaming had been perceived as discriminatory (Lau v. Nichols (1974) in the United States) and additional specialist provision was regarded as essential to equip ESL students to participate in the mainstream curriculum provision. In the 1990s Australia had made great strides in research, developing educational provision and training in ESL (McKay and Scarino, 1991; NLLIA, 1993; Breen *et al*, 1997; McKay *et al,* 1997).

Mainstreaming, one could argue, was intended to provide EAL learners with the opportunities to continue learning with their peer group, promote mutual respect and understanding of linguistic and cultural diversity and provide communicatively purposeful opportunities for language learning. It has also become synonymous with locating EAL pupils physically within the classroom, not always with the appropriate support for either teacher or learner to optimise the language and learning possibilities. Mainstreaming has also been justified as securing 'equal access' to the curriculum for EAL learners. But what does this mean?

In her discussion of the concept of equality, Lynch states that a minimal conception of equality is defined in terms of 'equal formal rights and opportunities and is a central component of equality of access' (Lynch, 1999, p. 289). She states that basic equality is important in prohibiting fundamental abuses of human rights, and in 'challenging racial, ethnic, sexual or social supremacism' (*ibid*. p. 288). But she argues that it does not go far enough in enabling and encouraging different social groups to participate in society – in providing 'equality of participation'. Nor does it offer 'equality of condition', which might be perceived as an ideal state which gives equality of living conditions to all its members (*ibid.* p. 301). So Lynch sees conceptualisations of equality as belonging to a continuum, from the basic *equality of access* at one end to *equality of condition* at the other end. As she says, the problem does not reside with the marginalised group or the individual, but with institutions and systems. She goes on to say that basic equality or 'equality of formal rights and opportunities has little impact on the promotion of equality in any substantive sense. Substantive equality depends not simply on having the formal right to participate but on having the actual ability and resources to exercise that right, that is by being able to participate' (*ibid.* p. 291). And so she argues for equality of participation, that is 'ensuring that basic material needs and the basic psychological, educational and other needs of the target group are met so that they are in a position to participate on equal terms' (*ibid.*). This view is reflected in the findings of the Lau v. Nichols case (1974), which resulted in the establishment of the statutory right to specialist provision for ESL students in the United States.

EAL provision in England meets the definition of equality of access but does not necessarily provide equality of participation. EAL teaching and learning has taken a different direction and has been located firmly within a mainstream English curriculum with only discretionary funding for additional support for EAL learners. The premise throughout the last decade has been that this would be sufficient to meet the needs of language learning, social and cultural inclusion and equality of access.

But this adherence to a practice that has basically remained unchallenged in the last decade, which has delayed acknowledgement of the distinctiveness of EAL learning and EAL teachers' knowledge and skills, has perhaps unwittingly suited other educational thinking and initiatives, such as 'inclusion'. The debate regarding 'inclusion' has often been seen as referring primarily to special educational needs (SEN) and the inclusion of learners with learning difficulties within mainstream schools. Like EAL learners, SEN learners are expected to follow the national curriculum, and over the past decade the movement has gained momentum, for educational, ideological and financial reasons, to reduce specialist provision and locate more SEN pupils with a range of needs within local provision. The word 'inclusive', like 'mainstreaming' and 'access' seemed to lose its intrinsic meaning as it increasingly became a rhetorical term meaning different things to different groups. This is not to say that the intent behind the use of such terms is not sincere and worth pursuing, but rather that the particularity of the needs of certain groups of learners may be lost in the generality of the debate.

A future agenda

How will EAL provision reposition itself? Firstly there is a need to understand the context in which EAL teachers have been working in the past decade, that is, a context in which the specialism has been subsumed under the wider notion of equal access and mainstreaming. This position has not secured the academic success and achievements that one would wish for linguistic and ethnic minority pupils. Nor is it a time to posit the counter-notion that if we had enough specialist EAL teachers, the issues of raising achievement and securing equality of participation would be resolved. The polarising of the debate needs to be jettisoned. Teachers need to come to terms with the tensions that will persist between the specialist role required to address the individual needs of EAL learners and the wider role that strives to make mainstream pedagogy more inclusive of these learners. The profession needs to understand that it not an 'either/or' situation but a changing context in which a range of pedagogies is necessary.

If EAL teachers are to respond flexibly to the needs of individual learners, and if they are to engage more proactively with mainstream pedagogy to enable inclusion – culturally, linguistically and cognitively – then they will need an informed professional knowledge base afforded by opportunities for further professional development and for debating and researching the issues. They must also continue to engage with and challenge government policies that view equality and access to the curriculum for EAL learners from a minimalist position, as the mere presence of EAL learners in the classroom.

10

Debates around EMAG: rhetoric and reality

Catherine Wallace

T his chapter brings together some of the issues which surround the educational provision for EAL and ethnic minority groups, looking in particular at the gaps between rhetoric and reality. At the same time I revisit the issues raised in earlier chapters. First I review the historical background to the current EMAG initiative before going on to consider the particular groups affected by the policy, the implications for practice and the way forward.

Historical background
Hugh South in his chapter takes us through the historical phases of the development towards the current EMAG. Charlotte Franson, as she repositions and analyses this debate, offers a critical commentary on this history, noting some of its ironies and inconsistencies. A historical account of provision might take us even further back than Franson and South have, to the early days of phenomena such as bussing. The famous example of this assimilationist policy was played out in the 1960s in the London Borough of Ealing through the movement of quite large numbers of children, referred to then as immigrants, to schools in different parts of the borough. This kind of dispersal was well intentioned, and was designed to avoid ghetto schools – as well as, it must be said, to allay the anxieties of white parents.

Such assimilationist policies gave way towards the end of the 1970s to integrationist policies, which gave greater visibility to the languages and cultures of ethnic minority children. This phase in turn evolved into what came to be known as a pluralistic model, which acknowledged the presence and value of a range of linguistic and cultural practices, all of equal legitimacy, in contemporary multicultural societies.

Running alongside such policy debates was a further one on mainstreaming. During the relatively early days of extensive migration, from the Indian subcontinent in particular, children were withdrawn, either to specific classes or to language centres. Although this 'gulag' approach later became discredited, it must be said that its effectiveness very much depended, as always, on the nature of the teaching centres themselves. Many deplored, for instance, the passing of the Pathway Further Education Centre in Southall, specifically set up to meet the needs of the substantial number of young people who came to schooling in Britain in their mid to late teens. As a centre exclusively for second language learners, it was certainly not mainstream provision but it was widely admired as a well-resourced and well-staffed place of study which produced excellent results. I mention this to make the point that it is not necessarily the *type* of provision offered which should concern us but the *quality*. For, as Charlotte Franson notes in her chapter, merely to mainstream children with inadequate attention to their individual needs may satisfy conditions of equality of access but not of equality of participation. Thus care is needed when we interpret and evaluate the phases of provision for children with EAL, in particular the assumption, frequently aired, that we have moved away from the bad old days of withdrawal to the enlightened practice of mainstreaming.

The structures of provision are certainly important but ultimately our concern needs to be with the actual opportunities for learning provided to linguistic and ethnic minority children rather than with the ideological discourses surrounding them. The favoured current term is 'inclusion' but much the same caution needs to be exercised as with the term 'mainstreaming'. Inclusion means little if it is not accompanied by meaningful opportunities to participate fully in learning opportunities in school. As Roger West says in his chapter, including children does not mean merely not withdrawing them Certainly we should always be wary of separate provision, of educational apartheid, especially when it is offered to people of perceived low status. But we need to be equally cautious, as Franson argues, of unplanned integration, which may turn into unplanned assimilation.

In short, in looking at this field retrospectively, over time, one is bound to wonder if debates about terminology have tended to replace discussion of more substantial educational matters. We might ask what happened to the debates about the nature of the curriculum itself: issues which exercised us in the 1980s about the overwhelmingly white images and the institutionalised racism embedded in the discourses of school textbooks. Do teachers feel that we have now achieved inclusiveness through our materials, so that all children feel that their identities are acknowledged and their histories made known?

Similar issues are raised by the analysis of educational policy and its relation to broader social policy. Multiculturalism gave way to anti-racist perspectives which in turn lost favour largely because, as Paul Gilroy puts it, of the 'dictatorial character of antiracism', particularly in local government (Gilroy, 1992, p. 49). Academics have now moved on to talk of 'critical multiculturalism' or 'reflective multi-culturalism' (e.g. Rattansi, 1999), which looks at ethnic identity as interwoven with other kinds of identities. For example, Stuart Hall talks of the 'new ethnicities' as a way of reflecting the more complex cultural and racial identities of today's young people (Hall, 1992). And yet many of these interesting debates tend to circulate in the rarified world of academics, so that teachers may not always get the chance to reflect on their practical implications through, for instance, publications such as the journal *Multicultural Teaching*.

Policy
It is important to remind ourselves that the brief of EMAG is much wider than the remit covered by the old Section 11. Section 11 money was originally targeted at second-language learners from Commonwealth countries, later being also made available to serve

the needs of other non-Commonwealth new arrivals for whom English was a second or additional language. Issues of language learning were understandably salient. But when the area of concern is extended to include children whose mother tongue is English, if not necessarily a standard variety of English, EAL becomes considerably less important than issues of achievement and, in particular, of underachievement.

This clearly creates difficulties for the group of professionals, many represented in this book, who come from EAL backgrounds, and who see themselves primarily as language teachers. Within schools it is likely to be EAL teachers, many originally employed under the old Section 11, who will take on the EMAG responsibility. The status and role of many of these was already insecure, as Charlotte Franson notes; it is likely that with a wider brief this confusion and uncertainty will grow. Moreover, local authorities will make different kinds of policy decisions in an effort to adhere to the spirit of the new initiative. Many will vire most EMAG funding to individual schools. This may offer schools greater autonomy but will also present dilemmas and responsibilities that schools may not feel competent to shoulder. For this reason, Hugh South in his chapter doubts the value of massive virement to schools. Questions which arise over virement to schools are: whose responsibility is EMAG, a single named individual's – the EMAG co-ordinator – or is it a whole-school policy? Certainly in a primary school with which I am familiar, the EMAG co-ordinator, while grateful for the opportunity offered by increased funds for training, feels the weight of this responsibility.

Her dilemma may not be an uncommon one: she articulates it thus. With the new emphasis on specified children who are underachieving, she is aware of several African-Caribbean boys whom she would like specifically to track in order to uncover some of their likely difficulties. Extra resources could help her do this. However, the head-teacher sees this issue as beginning with behaviour problems. If resources are used in the first instance to tackle behaviour then, it is argued, the boys can settle down to learn. These are not-untypical sensitive points of dispute which are bound to arise with new initiatives, reflecting some uncertainty about roles and goals and exactly which groups, and groups within larger groups, should be targeted as at risk of underachievement.

Which groups?

It is crucial to differentiate the groups at risk of underachieving because the causes, circumstances and effects will be different. In some cases behavioural issues will lead to exclusion from class or school; in others, home circumstances may mean that it is hard to maintain progress. The Traveller's group comes to mind here. And within this group, as Kalwant Bhopal points out in her chapter, there are sub-groups whose circumstances will be different. In the case of the Gypsy Traveller group which she observed within primary and secondary schools, a major factor was the provision of support for homework and for travel arrangements. The practical goals of ensuring that children attended school regularly and had strong support within and outside school was crucial. These issues persist, although they will no longer be the concern of EMAG.

When we come to look in particular at children for whom English is a second language, including the newer arrivals, it is again necessary to discriminate between them in order to assess and address their needs adequately. It is clearly important that the children's mother tongue should be acknowledged and supported in schools. The confidence and sense of identity which follow from bilingualism and biliteracy, even with very young children, is well documented by Kenner (2000) and there is now long standing evidence, beginning with the work of Cummins in 1979, that additive bilingualism, where a second language is added to a strongly based first one, is a powerful resource for language development and learning. The success of linguistically sophisticated minority groups continues to testify to this.

However, as we must acknowledge if we are to accept the lessons of some cases of underachievement, not all bilingual children are in a position to make use of their bilingualism as a resource. First, I would argue that vague sentiments about the value of using the mother tongue are not enough. We need to investigate just what the role of the mother tongue is – including non-standard varieties of English in the case of some children – in order to do justice to the rich resources of children, and to avoid taking a romanticised view of minority languages or language varieties as exotic.

In short, the celebration of diversity is not enough. This is the value of research such as that of Raymonde Sneddon (forthcoming) who, in her study of Gujarati families in North London, noted how the close links with a local Gujarati Community Centre led to children maintaining relatively high levels of linguistic vitality in their home languages of Gujarati and Urdu, which seemed to support higher than average achievements in English language literacy at the age of eleven. As well as looking more closely at the role of the mother tongue in specific circumstances, we need to acknowledge that some children will not have the same access to English, in particular in homes where parents speak limited English, perhaps in preference to a stronger shared home language. Children might not readily acquire access to a wide range of genres and registers in English. In short, more fine-grained study of particular social, ethnic and language groups, of the kind carried out by Sneddon, would help us to target the needs of children more closely and offer a firmer grounding to our understanding of the circumstances underpinning not just under-achievement but, in many cases, high achievement.

Achievement

The emphasis on achievement, or rather, on underachievement, is crucial to EMAG. This is particularly difficult when the causes of underachievement remain unclear. One might argue that when it was a matter of language proficiency, low achievement could be related readily to difficulties with English at the formal level of grammar, pronunciation and vocabulary. In the early days of the immigration of children who were clearly new to English, the EAL brief was relatively simple. One might take issue with the methodologies favoured and certainly with the total neglect of the mother tongue, but the learning of English had clear priority. Causes of under-achievement become much more contentious when we are talking of children from ethnic minority backgrounds who were born here – even more so when the brief widens to include children of African-

Caribbean descent and from Gypsy Traveller communities. As I comment above, for them English is not a second language though, as Leung and his colleagues note, the typical language of school may represent a clear departure from the language varieties they are most familiar with (Leung *et al,* 1997). Hence the importance of differentiating between different groups of children; one group which will gain new emphasis under EMAG will be that described by Leung and colleagues as pupils born and brought up in Britain who are competent and confident users of local British vernacular 'Englishes' and entirely familiar with contemporary British cultural and educational practices but have difficulties in reproducing accurate and fluent written standard English in the preferred genres favoured in specific school disciplines (Leung and Harris, 1997, p.10).

Although we have tended to avoid the term disadvantage because of its associations with essentialist notions of deficit, it is hard, in the discussion of achievement and underachievement, to avoid the conclusion that schools are implicated in the disadvantaging of some groups of children. What has triggered the wording of the EMAG initiative is that certain groups are doing less well than others in tests and examinations. As Cummins notes, it seems probable that a variety of causal factors interact at the broader societal level in determining patterns of educational attainment (Cummins, 1996a, p. 7). Nonetheless, Gillborn and Gipps, looking at performance at GCSE, found that although the situation was too varied to talk of simple Black underachievement, because there was a different picture from LEA to LEA, African-Caribbean pupils were generally less successful than their Asian and white peers (Gillborn and Gipps, 1996, p. 28). In support of their findings, in one LEA with which I am familiar I was told, informally, that testing on school entry showed that children from certain ethnic minorities, such as African-Caribbean children, are doing at least as well as their white peers. However, as I was told by one EMAG teacher in the same LEA, the advantage quickly disappears.

We are familiar with the way in which initial disadvantage can be compounded in schools; even more troubling is the way that initial parity – or even advantage – is turned to disadvantage. These are clearly cases of school-induced underachievement. Moreover it is important to emphasise that many linguistic and ethnic minority children may be fairly high achievers who are capable of doing still better than they are. For when we talk of underachievement, this should not be taken to refer only to currently low-achieving children. Experienced teachers in the early years will point to Black and Asian children as among the highest achievers in their classes. This was the case with two schools I recently visited. Among a class of four-year-olds an African-Caribbean boy was much the best in the class; in another school with a majority of white children, in a Year 2 class, the teacher confided that the six highest achievers in her group were mixed race, African-Caribbean or Asian.

Practices and practice

This book is called *Making EMAG Work*, so we need to consider what kinds of practices surround the schooling of minority children and what kind of practice characterises classroom teaching. It is worth beginning with practices, because ways of doing things at whole-school level are likely to impact at classroom level. It is also worth reminding ourselves that it is not policies but practices which empower or exclude children. There may, for instance, be school characteristics which unwittingly discriminate against certain children. There may indeed be examples of institutional racism. We should not forget that a major trigger for the EMAG initiative was the Macpherson Report, following the Lawrence murder inquiry, which revealed institutional racism within the police service and invited scrutiny of other public services; schools are inevitably not immune from discriminatory practices. These are rarely caused by individual prejudice but are due to long-established conventions and structures which cumulatively disadvantage certain groups of children. Angela Creese in her chapter offers one example of this when she talks about whether the EAL/EMAG teacher is seen as support teacher or partner within the school. If the teacher is seen as support – and in primary schools the term support-teacher is common – then an opportunity is missed for a whole-class approach to language diversity and to the differentiation of tasks. This is not to deny that there is a place for teachers as support to individual learners; but if this is the only visible role for EAL/EMAG staff those teachers will tend to have lower status, and an opportunity will be missed to address curricular and language issues which concern whole classes, including mainstream learners.

There are other, possibly more serious, structural issues which contribute to disadvantaging minority children. We need to ask, for instance, how far it is still the case that EAL children, especially new arrivals with no proficiency in English, and children with behaviour problems, are assigned to special-needs provision. Roger West pursues this point in his discussion of the marginalisation of children with EAL. And Gillborn and Youdell report that in their conversations with teachers they noted that issues of EAL and SEN support are often run together, suggesting that organisationally the needs of such pupils are not always identified separately (Gillborn and Youdell, 2000, p. 75). The conflation of EAL with low ability needs to be strongly resisted.

When we come to classrooms themselves, they are certainly constrained by school structures and practices which are to some degree beyond the control of individual teachers. Yet there is still much the individual teacher can do to ensure not just equality of access but equality of participation. As Cummins points out, we as teachers can consider what kinds of classroom interactions will promote academic success for all students regardless of class, race or cultural background (Cummins, 1996a, p. 7). Also, in research terms, there is a need for classroom ethnographies, which look closely at conditions within classrooms which facilitate or frustrate the language development and learning of some children, in ways that we, as teachers absorbed in our own everyday practice, may not always realise.

It is worth looking particularly at literacy and language in connection with the needs of ethnic minority and bilingual children, especially now that, along with the numeracy strategy, the national literacy strategy (NLS) is playing such a major role in the life of schools. The Literacy Hour offers particular challenges but also new opportunities for EAL and EMAG teachers to exercise their professional knowledge, in order to offer access to linguistic and ethnic minority children. This is where their special expertise can be put to use. As language specialists, they may be in a better position than the class teachers to make proper assessments about whether a learner's difficulty with reading or writing is related to slow development or some kind of special need, or – as is most often the case – to the fact that the reading material is not supportive of the learner's current stage of language development.

Maggie Gravelle writes, in her chapter, about specific learners being misdiagnosed as having special needs or given inappropriate kinds of support with reading. As I have noted elsewhere, phonics instruction can be particularly mystifying for EAL learners (Wallace, 1988, 1992); equally so for speakers of non-standard varieties of English. This is not acknowledged in the NLS documents, where there is strong emphasis on phonics. There is little or no regard for the fact that for many children most familiar with non-standard 'Englishes' or children who are not native speakers of English, there will be systematic differences between their variety of English (or, if developing users of English, their current interlanguage) and the sounds or phonemes practiced in phonics work, which are based on Received Pronunciation. However what is useful for such learners is the development of print awareness. Here there is evidence that the much greater level of metalanguage included in the NLS because it makes explicit the visual features of print – terminology such as 'speech marks', 'capital letters', 'spaces' – is particularly useful for EAL learners. This kind of work draws attention to the manner in which speaking differs from writing and offers a bridge between children's current varieties of spoken English and the more fully structured nature of written English. Drawing attention to these visual features, visible as marks on the page, in the way that phonemes – a highly abstract concept – are not, supports the move of EAL children into the new medium of print. It is these kinds of insights into the relationship between learner's language systems and the language of learning about which language specialists are best able to advise class teachers.

If we look more generally at the Literacy Hour and its organisation, how are the needs of ethnic minority and EAL children catered for? First, in a positive spirit, there is evidence that the guided whole-class work of the first phase of the Literacy Hour is able to offer opportunities for children whose English is still insecure to take part in the oral work as and when they feel most comfortable, offering them space gradually to increase their participation. Difficulties seem to arise, as Maggie Gravelle points out, during the independent work. She notes that the tasks devised showed no evidence of having been planned with the needs of bilingual learners in mind – and this is serious cause for concern. It would seem that this is an area where greater thought is needed; that is, ways must be devised of ensuring participation in the curriculum through adjusting either the task or the text for children with limited English. This may also involve challenging long-held shibboleths such as 'the silent period'. As Roger West points out here, children learn not through silence but through engagement in interactions.

Concluding comments

Making EMAG work means teachers doing more than just following prescriptions as trainees on courses, useful as these are as prepara-tion for policy and curriculum change. It means exercising judg-ments which are informed by knowledge about language develop-ment and use, understanding the complex circumstances of dis-advantage, and appreciating the tensions between an increasingly acknowledged multicultural society and residual and deep-rooted racism in some communities (cf. Hewitt, 1996). A tall order. More-over, there is evidence that with the demise of the excellent RSA diploma in Teaching Language Across the Curriculum in Multi-cultural Schools, there has been a severe loss of expertise. Through no fault of their own, teachers taking on the EMAG role in their schools may lack professional preparation. One irony of the main-streaming discourse, as Charlotte Franson notes here, is that there is less of a role for the EAL teacher as specialist. If ethnic minority children's needs can be met within mainstream classes, albeit with the help of an EAL support teacher in the room, the requirement of a degree of specialist knowledge may be less readily acknowledged.

I should like to conclude with a plea for extending and enriching the role of EMAG advisers. I see two strands to this, both of which involve the deployment of expert knowledge. One is the whole-school role, in which all teachers in a school might consult such a key adviser about possible discriminatory practice across the school. The other is the need to acknowledge the value of having a professional who has a particular body of knowledge about language and learning development, over and above that possessed by mainstream teachers. If these conditions are established, EMAG staff would be seen not as sidelined but as possessing knowledge of wider issues relating to causes of underachievement as well as specific knowledge about language development. In this second role they could, moreover, advise on such matters as the difficulties likely to be caused by literacy materials; they could offer more confident diagnoses about why some children appear to be developing less successfully as readers and writers than their overall ability might suggest. Lacking well-grounded knowledge within schools, it is, as Franson points out, easy to fall back on orthodoxies which leave us with an empty and unhelpful set of polarities. Talk of inclusion, withdrawal and mainstreaming and of underachievement, with little or no analysis of what these processes mean, fails to address the needs of learners in practical ways.

We need to bring reality to rhetoric. Doing so means bringing EAL and EMAG teachers from the margins, along with their learners, through an acknowledgement of the value of their professional role. Of course, making EMAG work will also be the responsibility of LEAs, as Peter Nathan documents in his chapter. Finally, however, it is up to schools and teachers to work towards the greater inclusiveness of currently underachieving children, through close investigation of the structures, practices and teaching within their own school settings.

Notes

1. See, for example, Cummins (1996b) and Blackledge (2000) for a discussion of empowerment in relation to schooling and to literacy.

2. For example, in 1999-2000, QCA, the TTA, OFSTED and the DfEE have all contributed significant publications relating to raising the attainment of ethnic minority pupils.

3. See NALDIC (1999) for a fuller list of pupil variables and Spolsky (1989) for a more academic discussion of learner variables.

4. For further discussion see, for example, Rampton (1995) and Leung, Harris and Rampton (1997).

5. The government responded to the publication of the Gillborn and Gipps report with a 'ten point plan'. This 'plan' included a new emphasis on ethnic monitoring, action by QCA, OFSTED and the TTA, and commissioning a research project to look at successful schools. It also led to the setting up of a task group on Raising Achievement of Ethnic Minority Pupils, since disbanded by the Labour government.

6. For more details on these groups see Jill Rutter's chapter on refugee children and Crispin Jones' chapter on Turkish Cypriot children. For more details on Somali children see Ali and Jones (2000).

7. See NALDIC and NASSEA (1996) for examples.

8. At a meeting with a joint NALDIC and NASSEA delegation, Under-Secretary of State, Charles Clarke, is reported as saying that he 'believed that devolution was about schools taking on full responsibility for all their pupils, and that changes in Section 11 provision should be a proxy for the kind of transformation in the school system which he would like to take place.' (*NALDIC News* 16, November 1998, p. 24)

9. It was claimed, for example, that Section 11 funding was being used to pay for teachers whose role in schools was indistinguishable from mainstream class or subject teachers. Communities and others therefore argued that the funding was being used for general educational purposes and not as additional funding to support the achievement of ethnic minority pupils.

10. The guidance given in the Supplement to Circular 13/98 *The Standards Fund 1999-2000* refers only to schools 'establishing a policy ' in relation to the grant.

11. Chapter two is based on a presentation made at the Institute of Education in December 1999 in which the author was very upbeat about the positive features of the new funding regime.

12. A good summary of the clouded history of Section 11 can be found in 'A Comedy of Errors' by Dorn and Hibbert in Troyna's *Race, Inequality and Education* (1987).

13. This chapter was written before the proposed changes to the Schools Standards Fund, of which EMAG forms a part.

14. Section 11 also funded some LEA-organised English language teaching for adult refugees and asylum-seekers.

15. International Centre for Intercultural Studies (ICIS) (1999) *Turkish Cypriot Children in London Schools*.

16. Underperformance using current government indicators is obviously a crude tool for looking at inner city educational performance. Until value added factors are reliably incorporated, many current Government statistics reveal rather less than they appear to.

17. A notable exception to this was Monica Taylor's report on the community for the Swann Committee (Taylor, 1988). See also Angela Creese's fascinating 1998 study (Creese, 1997).

18. Readers wishing to join the list can usually get details from their LEA EMAG co-ordinator.

19. Recently, the term 'Travellers' has become an acceptable term to describe a number of distinct communities who are or have been associated with a nomadic lifestyle. This includes Gypsies/Romanies of English, Scottish or Welsh heritage; Gypsies and Travellers of Irish heritage; Roma/Gypsies mainly from Eastern and Central Europe; Fairground families or Show people; Circus families; New Travellers and Bargees. For this chapter, as for the research report, the research team have used the term 'Gypsy Traveller' to represent the main group who participated in the research.

20. For a detailed discussion of the findings, see Bhopal *et al*, 2000.

21. See Bhopal *et al*, 2000 for more details of the research methodology adopted.

22. The larger study from which this chapter draws used the ethnography of communication (Hymes, 1968, 1972) and micro-ethnographic analysis (Erickson, 1996) for its theoretical and methodological framework.

23. All the schools involved had previously had the support of Section 11 staff and bilingual assistants and many of them continue to offer a similar, although sometimes reduced, level of classroom support.

24. The consultation on English in the national curriculum, popularly known as *The Cox Report* devoted a chapter to the needs of bilingual learners.

25. See Chapter Two in Dulay *et al,* 1982, for a discussion of the language learning environment. Note however, that much of the work was written with reference to adult learners.

26. A DfEE funded project between NALDIC, the University of Birmingham and BIELT (British Institute for English Language Teaching) April 2000.

Bibliography

Ali, E. and Jones, C. (2000) *Somali Children in Camden Schools*. London: Camden LEA.

Alibhai-Brown, J. (2000) 'Be at ease in your own skin'. *Times Educational Supplement,* May 12, 2000, p. 28.

Ball, S. (1990) *Politics and Policy-making in Education: Explorations in Policy Sociology*. London: Routledge.

Beard, R. (1999) *National Literacy Strategy: Review of Research and other Related Evidence*. London: DfEE.

Bhopal, K. (forthcoming) *Working Towards Inclusive Education: Aspects of Good Practice for Gypsy Traveller Pupils*. London: DfEE.

Billig, M. (ed.) (1988) *Ideological Dilemmas*. London: Sage Publications.

Blackledge, A. (2000) *Literacy, Power and Social Justice*. Stoke on Trent: Trentham Books.

Blair, M. and Bourne, J. (1998) *Making the Difference: Teaching and Learning Strategies in Successful Multi-ethnic Schools*. London:DfEE.

Bolloten, B and Spafford, T. (1998) 'Supporting refugee children in East London primary schools' in Jones, C. and Rutter, J. (eds.) *Refugee Education: Mapping the Field*. Stoke on Trent: Trentham Books.

Bourne, J. (1989) *Moving into the Mainstream*. Windsor: NFER-Nelson.

Bourne, J. and McPake, J. (1991) *Partnership Teaching: co-operative teaching strategies for language support in multilingual classrooms*. London: HMSO.

Breen, M., Barratt-Pugh, C., Derewianka, B., House, H., Hudson, C., Lumley, T. and Rohl, M. (1997) *Profiling ESL Children: How Teachers Interpret and Use National and State Assessment Frameworks*. Canberra: Department of Employment, Education, Training and Youth Affairs.

Brennan, C. and Taylor, I. (1998) 'Case Studies of Bilingual Readers'. *Primary Teaching Studies*, vol. 10, no. 1.

British Refugee Council (1987) *Asylum Statistics*. London: British Refugee Council.

Central Advisory Council for Education (England) (1967) *Children and their Primary Schools [The Plowdon Report]* (2 volumes). London: HMSO.

Commission for Racial Equality (CRE) (1986) *The Teaching of English as a Second Language*. London: HMSO.

Coulby, D. and Jones, C. (1996), 'Post-modernity, education and European identities'. *Comparative Education, vol.* 32, pp. 171-184.

Cox, B (1998) *Literacy is Not Enough*. Manchester: Manchester University Press.

Creese. A. (1997) Mainstreaming as Language Policy and Classroom Practice: Partner Teachers' Roles, Relationships and Talk in Multilingual British Secondary Schools. (unpublished doctoral dissertation). University of Pennsylvania.

Creese, A. and Hey, V. with Daniels, H., Fielding, S., Leonard, D. and Smith, M. (forthcoming). *Within firing range? targeting the performance of gender.* London: Taylor and Francis

Cummins, J. (1979) 'Linguistic Interdependence and the Educational Development of Bilingual Children'. *Review of Educational Research,* vol. 49, pp. 222-251.

Cummins, J. (1996a) 'Negotiating identities in the classroom and society'. *Multicultural Teaching* vol. 15, no. 1.

Cummins, J. (1996b) *Negotiating Identities: Education for Empowerment in a Diverse Society*. Ontario: CABE.

Dale, R. and Ozga, J. (1991) *Understanding Education Policy: Principles and Perspectives*. Milton Keynes: Open University Press.

Davison, C. (1993) 'Integrating ESL into the Mainstream: Australian Perspectives'. *Multicultural Teaching*. vol 11, no 3.

DES (Department of Education and Science) (1972) *The Continuing Needs of Immigrants*. (Education Survey 14). London: HMSO.

DES (Department of Education and Science) (1975) *A Language for Life* (The Bullock Report). London: HMSO.

DES (Department of Education and Science) (1983) *The Education of Traveller Children*: *A Discussion Paper*. London: HMSO

DES (Department of Education and Science) (1985), *Education for All: Final Report of the Committee of Inquiry into the Education of Children from Ethnic Minority Groups* (The Swann Report). London: HMSO.

DES and the Welsh Office (1989) *English for Ages* 5-16. (The Cox Report). London: HMSO.

DES and the Welsh Office (1990) *English in the National Curriculum*. London: HMSO.

DfEE (1998a) *Supplement to Circular 13/98 The Standards Fund 1999-2000. Letter to Chief Education Officers*. London: DfEE.

DfEE (1998b) *Ethnic Minority Achievement Grant*: *Supplement to the Circular 13/98*. www.dfee.gov.uk (accessed July. 2000).

DfEE (1998c) Requirements for Courses of Initial Teacher Training: Standards for the Award of Qualified Teacher Status (Circular 4/98). www.dfee.gov.uk (accessed July 2000).

DfEE (1998d) *The National Literacy Strategy*. London: DfEE.

DfEE (1998e) Circular 13/98 – The Standards Fund 1999-2000. London: DfEE.

Dobson, J. (1999) *Pupil Mobility in Schools*. London: DfEE Publications.

Dorn, A. and Hibbert, P. (1987) 'A Comedy of Errors: ,Section 11 Funding and Education' in Troyna, B. (ed.) *Race, Inequality and Education*. London: CRE.

Dulay, H., Burt, M. and Krashen, S. (1982) *Language Two*. Oxford: Oxford University Press.

Edwards, V. (1983) *Languages in Multicultural Classrooms*. London: Batsford Ltd.

Edwards, V. and Redfern, A. (1992) *The World in a Classroom: Language in Education in Britain and Canada*. Clevedon: Multilingual Matters.

Erickson, F. (1996) 'Ethnographic microanalysis' in McKay, S. and Hornberger, N. (eds.) *Sociolinguistics and Language Teaching*. New York: Cambridge University Press. pp. 283-306.

Essex TES (1997) *Educational Opportunity for Secondary Age Gypsy/Traveller Pupils*. Colchester: Essex Traveller Education Service.

Franson, C. (1995) *The role of the English as a second/additional language support teacher: necessary conditions for a new definition*. (NALDIC Occasional Paper 3). Watford: NALDIC.

Gass, S. M., Mackey, A. and Pica, T. (1998) 'The role of input and interaction in second language acquisition: an introduction'. *The Modern Language Journal*. vol. 82, pp. 299-307.

Gee, J. P. (1999) *An Introduction to Discourse Analysis*. London and New York: Routledge.

Gibbons, P. (1991) *Learning to Learn in a Second Language*. Newtown, Australia: PETA.

Gillborn, D. and Gipps, C. (1996) *Recent Research on the Achievements of Ethnic Minority Pupils: OFSTED Review of Research*. London: HMSO.

Gillborn D. and Youdell D. (2000) *Rationing Education*. Buckingham: Open University Press.

Gilroy, P. (1992) 'The End of Antiracism' in Donald, J. and Rattansi, A. (eds.) *Race, Culture and Difference*. London: Sage.

Hall, S. (1992) 'New Ethnicities' in Donald, J and Rattansi, A (eds.) *Race, Culture and Difference*. London: Sage.

Harley, B. (1993) 'Instructional strategies and SLA in early French immersion'. *Studies in Second Language Acquisition*. vol. 15, pp. 245–259.

Harley, B. (ed.) (1995) *Lexical Issues in Language Learning*. Ann Arbor, Michigan: Research Club in Language Learning and John Benjamins.

Hatcher, R. and Troyna, B. (1994) 'The Policy Cycle: A Ball-by-Ball Account'. *Journal of Education Policy* vol. 9, no. 2.

Heighway, J. and Moxham, G. (1998) *A Study to Identify Potential Barriers that may exist for Traveller Children Progressing in their Education. Blackpool*, Lancashire and Blackburn with Darwen: Traveller Education Consortium.

Hewitt, R. (1996) *Routes of Racism*. Stoke on Trent: Trentham Books.

Hilton, M (1998) 'Raising Literacy Standards: The True Story'. *English in Education* vol. 32, no. 3.

Home Office (1989) *A Scrutiny of Grants Under Section 11 of the Local Government Act: Final Report*. London: HMSO.

Home Office (1990a) *Section 11 of the Local Government Act 1966. Grant Administration: Guidelines and Instructions (Annexe B)*. London: Home Office.

Home Office (1990b) *Section 11 of the Local Government Act. Grant Administration: Policy Criteria*. London: Home Office.

Hymes, D. (1968) 'The ethnography of speaking' in Fishman, J. (ed.) *Readings in the Sociology of Language*. The Hague: Moulton.

Hymes, D. (1972) 'On communicative competence' In Pride, J. and Holmes, J. (eds.) *Sociolinguistics*. Harmondsworth: Penguin.

ICIS (International Centre for Intercultural Studies) (1999) *Turkish Cypriot Children in London Schools* (a report for the Turkish Cypriot Forum). London: ICIS, Institute of Education.

Jones, C. and Rutter, J. (eds) (1998) *Refugee Education: Mapping the Field*. Stoke on Trent: Trentham Books.

Kiddle, C. (1999) *Traveller Children: A Voice for Themselves*. London: Jessica Kingsley.

Kress, G. (1995) 'Making Signs and Making Subjects: the English Curriculum and Social Futures'. An inaugural lecture delivered at the Institute of Education, University of London on 2nd March 1995.

Kress, G. (1996) 'English at the crossroads: rethinking curricula of communication in the context of the turn to the visual'. in Hawisher, G. and Selfe, C. (eds.) *Critical Reflections on Literacy and Technology: Confronting the Issues*. Urbana-Champaign: University of Illinois Press.

Jakobson, R. (1960) 'Linguistics and Poetics' in *Selected Writings II*. The Hague: Mouton.

Jakobson, R. (1971) 'Shifters, verbal categories, and the Russian verb' in *Selected Writings II*. The Hague: Mouton.

Jakobson, R. and Halle, M. (1975) *Fundamentals of Language*. The Hague: Mouton.

Johnson, R. (1991) 'My New Right Education' in *Education Unlimited: Schooling and Training and the New Right since 1979*. London: Unwin.

Kenner, C. (2000) H*ome Pages: Literacy links for bilingual children*. Stoke on Trent: Trentham Books.

Kerry, T. and Murdoch, A. (1993) 'Education managers as leaders: some thoughts on the context of the changing nature of schools'. *School Organisation* vol. 13, no.3.

Lee, A. (1997) 'Working Together? Academic literacies, co-production and professional partnerships'. *Literacy and Numeracy Studies* vol. 7, no. 2, pp. 65-82.

Leung, C. and Harris, R. (1997) *Language and Ethnic Minority Educational Achievement: Initiating a New Debate*. (Occasional Paper 11). Watford: NALDIC.

Leung, C., Harris, R. and Rampton, B. (1997) 'The idealised native-speaker: reified ethnicities and classroom realities'. TESOL *Quarterly, vol.* 31, no. 3, pp. 543-560.

Levine, J. (ed.) (1990) *Bilingual Learners and the Mainstream Curriculum*. London: Falmer.

Lo Bianco, J. (1999) *Policy, Globalisation and the Field of Bilingualism and English as an Additional Language*. Key-note address to NALDIC Conference, November 1999 (summarised in *EAL and Bilingualism: Policies for a New Agenda: Report of NALDIC's Annual Conference 1999*. Watford: NALDIC.)

Lodge, C. (1998) 'Working with Refugee Children: One Schools' Experience' in Jones, C. and Rutter, J. (eds.) *Refugee Education: Mapping the Field*. Stoke on Trent: Trentham Books.

Long, M. (1983) 'Native speaker/non-native speaker conversation and the negotiation of comprehensible input'. *Applied Linguistics*. vol. 4, no. 2, pp. 126-141.

Lynch, K. (1999) *Equality in Education*. Dublin: Gill and Macmillan.

McKay, P. and Scarino, A. (1991) *ESL Framework of Stages: An Approach to ESL Learning in Schools*. Carlton, Victoria: Curriculum Corporation.

McKay, P., Davies, A., Devlin, B., Clayton, J., Oliver, R. and Zammit, S. (1997) *The Bilingual Interface Project*. Canberra: Department of Employment, Education, Training and Youth Affairs.

Medwell, J., *et. al* (1998) *Effective Teachers of Literacy*. London: TTA.

Mehmet Ali, A. (1989) 'The Turkish community in Britain – some comments and observations on the immigration patterns, and legal and social position'. *Language Issues: Journal of NATESLA*. vol. 3, no. 1, pp. 19-23.

Mehmet Ali, A. (1991) 'The Turkish speech community' in Alladina, S. and Edwards, V. (eds.) *Multilingualism in the British Isles*. London: Longman.

Mehmet Ali, A. (1998) 'An unhappy experience'. *Adults Learning*, vol. 10, no. 2, pp. 11-13.

Mercer N. (1998) 'Development through dialogue: a socio-cultural perspective on the process of being educated'. in Quelhas, A. and Pereira, F. (eds.) *Cognition and Context*. Lisboa: Institute Superior de Psicologia Aplicada.

Mroz, M. Hardman, F. and Smith, F. (forthcoming) 'The Discourse of the Literacy Hour'. *Cambridge Journal of Education*.

NALDIC (1998a) *NALDIC News 16*. November 1998.

NALDIC (1998b) *Provision in Literacy Hours for Pupils Learning English as an Additional Language*. Watford: NALDIC.

NALDIC (1999) *NALDIC Working paper 5*, The distinctiveness of English as an additional language: a cross-curriculum discipline. Watford: NALDIC.

NALDIC and NASSEA (1996) *Policy for Funding Future provision for Ethnic Minority Pupils: a joint statement by NALDIC and NASSEA*. Watford: NALDIC.

NALDIC and NASSEA (1998) *Key Issues in the Current Debate about Section 11 Funding: A Discussion Paper for consideration by the Labour Government*. Watford: NALDIC.

NLLIA (1993) ESL Development: *Language and Literacy in Schools Project*. Canberra: National Languages and Literacy Institute of Australia.

NUT (1978) *Section 11: An NUT Report. London:* NUT.

OECD (1998) *Trends in International Migration*. Paris: OECD.

OFSTED (1996) *The Education of Travelling Children*. London: OFSTED.

OFSTED (1998) *The National Literacy Project*. London: OFSTED.

OFSTED (1999) *Raising the Attainment of Ethnic Minority Pupils: School and LEA Responses*. London: HMSO.

Pica, T. (1991) 'Classroom interaction, participation and comprehension: redefining relationships'. *System.* vol. 19, no. 3-4, pp. 437-452.

Pica, T. (1995) 'Teaching language and teaching language learners: the expanding roles and expectations of language teachers in communicative, content-based classrooms' in Alatis, J., Straehle, C., Gallenberger, B. and Ronkin, M. (eds.) *Linguistics and the Education of Language Teachers: Ethnolinguistic, Psycholinguistic, and Sociolinguistic Aspects.* (Georgetown University Round Table on Language and Linguistics). Washington DC: Georgetown University Press.

Power, S., Whitty, G. and Youdell, D. (1998) 'Refugees: Asylum-Seekers and the Housing Crisis' in Jones, C. and Rutter, J. (eds.) (1998) *Refugee Education: Mapping the Field.* Stoke on Trent: Trentham Books.

QCA (2000) *Developing the School Curriculum.* London: QCA.

Rampton, B. (1995) *Crossing: language and ethnicity among adolescents.* London: Longman.

Rattansi, A. (1999) 'Racism, Postmodernism and Reflexive Multiculturalism' In May, S. (ed.) *Critical Multiculturalism: Rethinking Multicultural and Antiracist Education* London: Taylor and Francis.

Refugee Council (1998) *Section 11 and Refugees.* Unpublished submission to the Home Office.

Reiss, C. (1975) *Education of Travelling Children.* Macmillan: London.

Ribbins, P. and Sherratt, B. (1997) *Radical Educational Policies and Conservative Secretaries of State.* London: Cassell.

Rowan, P. (2000) 'Hitting the target but missing the point'. *Times Educational Supplement*, 25 February 2000.

Ruiz, R. (1984) 'Orientations in language planning'. *National Association of Bilingual Educational Journal.* vol. 8, no. 2, pp. 15-34.

Rutter, J. (1994) *Refugee Children in the Classroom.* Stoke on Trent: Trentham Books.

Rutter, J. (forthcoming) *Supporting Refugee Children in 21st Century Britain:* a *compendium of essential information* (wholly revised edition). Stoke on Trent: Trentham Books.

SCAA (1996) *Teaching English as an Additional Language: A Framework for Policy.* London: SCAA.

Sealey, A. (1999) *Theories about language in the National Literacy Strategy,* Centre for Research in Elementary and Primary Education, University of Warwick.

Seidlhofer, B. (ed.), *Principles and Practice in Applied Linguistics: Studies in Honour of H. G. Widdowson.* Oxford: Oxford University Press.

Scardamalia, M. and Bereiter, C. (1999) *Schools as Knowledge Building Organizations.* http://csile.oise.utoronto.ca/abstracts/ciar-understanding.html (accessed July 2000).

Schmidt, R. (1990) 'The role of consciousness in second language acquisition'. *Applied Linguistics.* vol. 11, no. 2, pp. 17-46.

Sinclair, J., and Courthard, R. (1975) *Towards an analysis of discourse: the English used by teachers and pupils.* London: Oxford University Press.

Sneddon, R. (2000 forthcoming) 'Language and literacy practices in Gujarati Muslim families'. In Martin-Jones, M. and Jones, K. (eds.) *Multilingual Literacies: reading and writing different worlds.* London: Routledge.

Spolsky, B. (1989) *Conditions for Second language Learning.* Oxford: Oxford University Press.

Swain, M. (1985) 'Communicative competence: some roles of comprehensible input and comprehensible output in its development'. in Gass, S. and Madden, C. (eds.) *Input in second language acquisition.* Rowley, MA: Newbury House.

Taylor, M. (1988) *Worlds Apart? A Review of Research into the Education of Pupils of Cypriot, Italian, Ukrainian and Vietnamese Origin, Liverpool Blacks and Gypsies.* Windsor: NFER- Nelson.

Toohey, K. (1998) 'Breaking them Up, Taking Them Away': ESL Students in Grade 1'. *TESOL Quarterly,* vol. 32, no.1.

Tosi, A. and Leung, C. (eds.) (1999) *Rethinking Language Education: from a monolingual to a multilingual approach.* London: Royal Holloway, University of London and CILT.

UNHCR (United Nations High Commissioner for Refugees) (1997), 'The year in review'. *Refugee Magazine* vol. 3, pp. 1-31.

Vygotsky, L. (1986) *Thought and Language* (translated and edited by Alex Kozulin). Cambridge: MIT Press.

Wallace, C. (1988) *Learning to Read in a Multicultural Society: the social context of second language literacy.* London: Prentice Hall.

Wallace, C. (1992) *Reading.* Oxford: Oxford University Press.

West, R. (1998) *The Accidental Manager: new models for educational management* (Unpublished MA thesis). Institute of Education, London University.

Willett, J. (1995) 'Becoming First Graders in an L2: An Ethnographic Study of L2 Socialization'. *TESOL Quarterly* vol. 29, no. 3.

Worrall, D. (1979) *Gypsy Education: A Study of Provision in England and Wales.* Walsall: Walsall Council for Community Relations.

INDEX